Cooking
from the Coast
to the Cascades

Cooking
from the Coast
to the Cascades

Junior League of Eugene, Oregon

Cooking from the Coast to the Cascades

Library of Congress Number:
    2001 132199
ISBN: 0-9607976-2-9

Designed, Edited, and
Manufactured by
Favorite Recipes® Press
An imprint of

FRP

P.O. Box 305142
Nashville, Tennessee 37230
1-800-358-0560

Art Director: Steve Newman
Project Manager: Susan Larson

Manufactured in the
United States of America
First Printing: 2002   20,000 copies

Cookbook Committee

Chair
Melba Cunningham Detlefsen

Assistant Chair
Nancy Thompson

Vision
Diana Richardson

Theme
Diana Richardson
Peggy Schuurmans

Recipe Collection/Testing Coordinators
Kathy Pierce
Liz Gleim
Tanya Gregg
Laurel Allender
Kristin Kernutt
Nancy Grove
Paula Kongsore
Nancy Thompson

Non-Recipe Text Coordinators
Diana Richardson
Mary Sue Oldham
Jeannine Erving
Christina Lund
Lisa Korth

Chapter Chairs
Valley Mornings—Paula Kongsore
Let's Do Lunch—Laurel Allender
Weeknight Dinners—Tracey Webber
Coastal Getaways— Nancy Grove
Weekends in the Cascades —
        Kristin Kernutt
Vegetarian Lifestyles—Tanya Gregg
Special Occasions—Liz Gleim
Elegant Dinners—
        Melba Cunningham Detlefsen

Preliminary Chapter Selection
Kathy Pierce
Nancy Thompson
Liz Gleim

Marketing Coordinators
LaVonne Davis
George Maddox
Kathy Norman
Trina C. Radcliffe

Photography Selection, Design, and Cover
Cathi Cornils Busse
Daralyn DeHaven Murdoch
Jill King Niles

Special Thank Yous

Sustainers
Fran Curtis
Carol McCornack
Jan Petrie
Jan Shaver
Penny Carpenter Shephard
Kathleen Turner

The Oregon Wine Market
Oregon Trail Interpretive Center, Baker City
Caddis Fly Angling Shop
Berry Works
Doug Schultz
Matt Jarvis
Sacred Heart Guest House, Nancy Hager, Manager
Hazelnut Marketing Board
Gnass Photo Images
Frank Siegler

Special thanks to the Oregon Tourism Commission for supplying descriptive text of our beautiful state.

Professional Photography Credits

Bruce Berg
Back Cover Inset Photo: The rugged coastline in Southern Oregon at Bandon.

Bruce Berg was named Oregon's Professional Photographer of the Year in 1997, 1999 and 2000. He is among only 5 percent of professional photographers who have been named a Master Photographer and Photographic Craftsman by the Professional Photographers of America. His published works include a variety of magazines, calendars, and books, as well as *Travel Holiday* and the *World Book Encyclopedia*. View his award-winning web site at www.BruceBerg.com

Steve Terrill
Cover Photo: South Sister Mountain reflecting in Sparks Lake in the Deschutes National Forest, Oregon. Endsheets: Evening light glowing on evergreen trees and Haystack Rock at Cannon Beach, Oregon.

Photographer Steve Terrill is self-taught and has been trekking throughout the United States since 1980, seeking to preserve the grandeur of nature on film. To his credit, he has over seventeen books published to date. His work has appeared in numerous magazines and publications, including *Audubon*, *National Geographic*, *Travel & Leisure*, *Reader's Digest*, and *National Wildlife*. He can be e-mailed at terrillphoto@aol.com

Table of Contents

Our Junior League

Our Mission

The Junior League of Eugene is an organization of women committed to promoting volunteerism, developing the potential of women and improving the community through the effective action and leadership of trained volunteers. Its purpose is exclusively educational and charitable.

Our Members

The Junior League of Eugene reaches out to all women 21 years of age or older regardless of race, religion, color or national origin who demonstrate an interest in and commitment to volunteerism. More than 100 members donate 15,000 hours of community service annually.

Our Vision

The Junior League of Eugene strives to provide a community that values children and adolescents. All children will be safe and live in drug-free, stable, nurturing environments where basic needs of food, shelter, clothing, love and education are met.

Our Values

The Junior League of Eugene believes...
♦ Children are our greatest resource.
♦ The health and welfare of our children should be our main priority for a positive future. Every child deserves an equal opportunity for health care, education, food, shelter and sense of security.
♦ A physically and mentally healthy family is the best resource for child development.
♦ The development of leadership skills through the training of its members has a positive effect on the community.

Introduction

Cooking from the Coast to the Cascades promises to take you on a sensational journey from the majestic cliffs and local chowder houses on the coast to the pristine lakes and cozy cabins in the Cascade Mountains.

Imagine views of the green valleys from your terrace as you peruse the chapter on "Special Occasions." Visualize a hillside lush with grapevines as you select an Oregon wine from the helpful wine guide. Abundant, fresh produce will fill your basket as you shop for any of the delicious recipes from the "Let's Do Lunch" or "Vegetarian Lifestyles" chapters. Remembering the many different and unique types of berries, mushrooms, and nuts to be utilized is sure to make your menu fabulous. If fishing in one of the many lakes, rivers, or coastal bays makes you dream of grilled salmon or trout, then take a look at "Coastal Getaways" or "Weekends in the Cascades." These chapters are comprehensive enough to please even the pickiest of fish and seafood eaters.

Cooking from the Coast to the Cascades provides Oregon fare that is certain to please the palate as well as conjure up the images of Oregon's many scenic wonders.

Valley Mornings

Valley mornings encompass an array of poignant daydreams for those of us fortunate enough to call Oregon our home.

The anticipation of the day is rewarded by the sun rising over the trees and the misty fog breaking. Sipping fresh fruit smoothies and eating delicious coffee cake enrich the daybreak. An early-morning delight is breathing crisp, fresh air while sitting on a deck overlooking a tree-lined lake enjoying your Bloody Mary and a fabulous egg dish made with ingredients picked up at a local farmers' market. A morning in the valley is a lazy Sunday, wrapped in a blanket with a steaming cup of espresso and a slice of berry cake made with locally grown berries, while rain pelts the windows. Perhaps you step in the door after an early-morning run, smell the freshly brewed coffee mixed with aromas of cinnamon and bacon, and are aware two miles will not be adequate to burn off the meal you are about to joyfully consume.

The Willamette Valley is a treasure trove of culinary and sensory pleasures just waiting to be discovered. From berries, herbs, and fruits to locally roasted coffee beans and products from egg farms and dairies, there is something grown and produced here to please every palate.

Creswell Valley meets the lower Cascades in Lane County, Oregon

photo by Bruce Berg

Valley Mornings

Contents

Fresh Cranberry Bread

  2 cups sifted flour
  1 cup sugar
  1¹/₂ teaspoons baking powder
  1 teaspoon salt
  ¹/₂ teaspoon baking soda
  ¹/₄ cup (¹/₂ stick) butter or margarine
  1 egg, beaten
  1 teaspoon grated orange zest
  ³/₄ cup orange juice
  1¹/₂ cups light raisins or currants
  1¹/₂ cups fresh cranberries, chopped

Sift the flour, sugar, baking powder, salt and baking soda into a bowl. Cut in the butter until crumbly. Add the egg, orange zest and orange juice. Stir to mix well. Fold in the raisins and cranberries. Spoon into a greased loaf pan. Bake at 350 degrees for 1 hour and 10 minutes or until a wooden pick inserted in the center comes out clean. Remove to a wire rack to cool.

Yield: 1 loaf

Fresh Strawberry Bread

  1¹/₄ cups vegetable oil
  4 eggs
  2¹/₂ cups sliced fresh strawberries
  3 cups flour
  1 teaspoon baking soda
  1 teaspoon salt
  1¹/₂ teaspoons cinnamon
  2 cups sugar
  1¹/₂ cups chopped pecans

Beat the oil and eggs in a mixing bowl until fluffy. Fold in the strawberries. Mix the flour, baking soda, salt, cinnamon and sugar in a bowl. Stir the dry ingredients into the strawberry mixture. Stir in the pecans. Spoon into 2 greased and floured loaf pans. Bake at 325 degrees for 1 hour or until a wooden pick inserted in the center comes out clean. Remove to a wire rack to cool.

Yield: 2 loaves

Oatmeal Bread

1¼ cups milk
¼ cup (½ stick) butter or
    margarine
1 cup rolled oats
1 envelope quick-rising dry yeast
¼ cup (110-degree) water
⅓ cup pure maple syrup

1 egg
1½ teaspoons salt
¾ cup whole wheat flour
2 cups unbleached flour
½ cup currants or raisins
    (optional)
Rolled oats

Heat the milk in a saucepan. Pour the hot milk over the butter and 1 cup oats in a large mixing bowl. Stir to mix and let cool to lukewarm. Dissolve the yeast in the water in a small bowl. Add to the oat mixture. Add the maple syrup, egg, salt and whole wheat flour to the bowl. Beat at medium speed for 3 minutes. Stir in the unbleached flour gradually with a wooden spoon. Stir in the currants.

Grease a 2-pound coffee can or two 4x8-inch loaf pans. Sprinkle the can or pans with rolled oats to coat the bottom and sides. Spoon the dough into the prepared can or pans. Bake at 350 degrees for 40 to 45 minutes for the can or 25 minutes for the loaf pans. Remove to a wire rack to cool.

Yield: 1 can-size loaf or 2 loaves

French Breakfast Puffs

1½ cups flour
½ cup sugar
1½ teaspoons baking powder
¼ teaspoon nutmeg
⅛ teaspoon salt
1 egg, lightly beaten
½ cup milk

⅓ cup butter or margarine,
    melted
¼ cup sugar
½ teaspoon cinnamon
¼ cup (½ stick) butter or
    margarine, melted

Mix the flour, ½ cup sugar, baking powder, nutmeg and salt in a bowl. Make a well in the center. Mix the egg, the milk and ⅓ cup melted butter in a bowl. Pour the egg mixture into the well in the dry ingredients. Stir until just moistened. The batter may be lumpy. Fill lightly greased muffin cups ⅔ full with the batter. Bake at 350 degrees for 20 to 25 minutes or until golden brown.

Mix ¼ cup sugar and cinnamon in a shallow bowl. Dip the tops of the hot muffins into ¼ cup melted butter and then into the cinnamon-sugar until coated. Cool on a wire rack.

Yield: 12 muffins

Pumpkin Muffins

1^1/2 cups flour
1/2 cup sugar
2 teaspoons baking powder
1 teaspoon cinnamon
1/2 teaspoon ginger
1/4 teaspoon ground cloves
1/2 cup raisins
1 egg, slightly beaten
1/2 cup milk
1/2 cup canned pumpkin
1/4 cup (1/2 stick) butter or margarine, melted
2^1/2 teaspoons sugar
1/2 teaspoon cinnamon

Sift the flour, 1/2 cup sugar, baking powder, 1 teaspoon cinnamon, ginger and cloves in a bowl. Stir in the raisins. Mix the egg, milk, pumpkin and melted butter in a separate bowl. Add to the dry ingredients and stir until just mixed. Fill lightly greased muffin cups 2/3 full with the batter.

Mix 2^1/2 teaspoons sugar and 1/2 teaspoon cinnamon in a small bowl. Sprinkle on top of the unbaked muffins. Bake at 400 degrees for 20 to 25 minutes. Remove to a wire rack to cool.

Yield: 12 muffins

Willamette Valley

The Willamette Valley has perhaps the world's most diverse agriculture. The rich soil yields mass quantities of fruits, vegetables, flowers, herbs, hazelnuts, hops, holly and Christmas trees, mint, grass seeds, oats, as well as some of the world's finest pinot noir, pinot gris, chardonnay, and riesling grapes.

In April, blooming dogwood trees paint the understory of the forest a pale pink.

Sausage Muffins with Basil Honey

1/2 pound bulk pork or turkey sausage
2 cups flour
2 tablespoons sugar
1 tablespoon baking powder
1/4 teaspoon salt
1 cup milk
1 egg, slightly beaten
1/4 cup (1/2 stick) butter or margarine, melted
1/2 cup shredded Cheddar cheese
Basil Honey

Brown the sausage in a skillet until cooked through. Remove to paper towels to drain. Mix the flour, sugar, baking powder and salt in a bowl. Make a well in the center. Mix the milk, egg and melted butter in a small bowl. Pour into the well in the dry ingredients. Stir until just moistened. Stir in the drained sausage and Cheddar cheese until just mixed. Fill muffin cups coated with nonstick cooking spray 2/3 full with the batter. Bake at 350 degrees for 20 minutes or until golden brown. Remove to a wire rack. Drizzle immediately with Basil Honey.

Yield: 12 muffins

Basil Honey

1 cup honey
2 to 3 fresh basil leaves, chopped

Heat the honey in a small saucepan until warm. Place the basil in a jar with a tight-fitting lid. Pour the warm honey over the basil. Cover the jar and let stand for at least a week to blend the flavors.

Blueberry-Stuffed French Toast

12 slices homemade-style bread, crusts trimmed,
   cut into 1-inch cubes
16 ounces cream cheese, cut into 1-inch cubes
1 cup blueberries
12 eggs, beaten
2 cups milk
$^1/_3$ cup maple syrup
1 cup sugar
2 tablespoons cornstarch
1 cup water
1 cup blueberries

Arrange $^1/_2$ the bread cubes in a single layer in a buttered 9x11-inch baking pan. Arrange the cubes of cream cheese on top. Sprinkle with the 1 cup blueberries. Arrange the remaining bread cubes over the blueberries. Mix the eggs, milk and maple syrup in a bowl. Pour over the bread mixture. Cover with foil and chill overnight. Bake, covered, at 350 degrees for 30 minutes. Remove the foil and bake for 30 minutes or until puffy.

Mix the sugar, cornstarch and water in a saucepan. Cook over medium-high heat, stirring constantly, for 5 minutes or until thickened. Reduce the heat and stir in 1 cup blueberries. Simmer for 10 minutes. Serve with the hot French toast.

Yield: 6 servings

Hendricks Park

Strolling through the rhododendron gardens of Hendricks Park on Mother's Day is a tradition I savor every year. A dazzling rainbow of pink, orange, purple, red, white, and yellow rhododendrons and azaleas fill the park from floor to canopy. Azaleas, ferns, fuchsias, and peonies line trails that wander under old rhododendrons with trunks as big as trees.

My kids, with faces as bright as the flowers, race from bush to bush calling me, "Come look at this one, Mommy." With its fantastic full bloom in May, Hendricks Park is a perfect Mother's Day destination.

Oregon Griddle Cakes

2 cups flour
2 tablespoons baking powder
2 teaspoons sugar
1 teaspoon salt
2 cups milk
$^1/_2$ cup (1 stick) butter, melted, cooled
3 eggs

Mix the flour, baking powder, sugar and salt in a bowl. Stir in the milk and melted butter. Beat in the eggs 1 at a time. Let the batter stand for 30 minutes.

Pour a scant $^1/_4$ cup batter onto a medium-hot lightly greased griddle. Cook until bubbles appear and break. Turn the pancake. Cook until golden brown. Repeat with remaining batter. Serve hot with Oregon maple syrup.

Yield: 6 servings

Dutch Babies

4 eggs
1 cup milk
1 cup flour
1 teaspoon sugar
$^1/_3$ cup butter

Whip the eggs in a blender for 1 minute. Add the milk gradually, alternating with the flour and sugar. Blend for 2 minutes. Heat the butter in an ovenproof skillet until sizzling. Pour the batter into the skillet. Place the skillet in the oven and bake at 425 degrees for 20 minutes or until puffed. Serve with syrup, confectioners' sugar and fresh fruit.

Yield: 4 servings

Golden Delicious Apple Brunch Cake

2 cups chopped unpeeled Golden
    Delicious apples
1 egg
1 cup sugar
1/4 cup vegetable oil
1/2 teaspoon vanilla extract

1 cup flour
1 teaspoon cinnamon
1 teaspoon baking soda
1/2 cup chopped pecans
Confectioners' sugar

Mix the apples, egg, sugar, oil, vanilla, flour, cinnamon, baking soda and pecans in a bowl. The batter will be thick. Spoon into a 9-inch nonstick baking pan. Bake at 350 degrees for 45 minutes. Remove to a wire rack to cool. Dust with confectioners' sugar while still warm.

Yield: 8 servings

Blueberry Buttermilk Coffee Cake

1 cup buttermilk
2 eggs
2 teaspoons vanilla extract
1 1/2 teaspoons grated orange zest
2 cups flour
1 cup sugar
1 tablespoon baking powder
1/4 teaspoon nutmeg
1/2 cup (1 stick) cold unsalted
    butter, cut into pieces

1 1/2 cups frozen unsweetened
    blueberries
2/3 cup sugar
1/2 cup chopped pecans
2 tablespoons butter, melted
1 1/2 teaspoons cinnamon
1/2 teaspoon nutmeg

Whisk the buttermilk, eggs, vanilla and orange zest in a small bowl. Mix the flour, 1 cup sugar, baking powder and 1/4 teaspoon nutmeg in a large bowl. Rub the cold butter into the dry ingredients with fingers until the mixture resembles coarse meal. Stir in the buttermilk mixture. Fold in the blueberries. Pour the batter into a buttered 9-inch square baking pan. Mix the 2/3 cup sugar, pecans, melted butter, cinnamon and 1/2 teaspoon nutmeg in a bowl. Sprinkle on top of the unbaked cake. Bake at 350 degrees for 1 hour and 5 minutes. Cool on a wire rack.

Yield: 8 servings

Honeyed Oranges

3 large navel oranges, peeled, sliced crosswise
1/3 cup frozen orange juice concentrate, thawed
1/3 cup honey
Paprika (optional)

Divide the orange slices between 4 plates. Mix the orange juice concentrate and honey in a small bowl. Drizzle over the orange slices. Sprinkle with paprika.

Yield: 4 servings

Zucchini Custard Casserole

4 slices bacon
2 cups thinly sliced zucchini (about 3 medium)
1 large onion, finely chopped
2 to 3 garlic cloves, minced
6 eggs
3/4 teaspoon salt
1/2 teaspoon Italian seasoning
1 cup plain yogurt
2 cups cooked rice
1 cup shredded Cheddar cheese

Cook the bacon in a skillet over medium heat until crisp. Remove to paper towels to drain. Crumble when cool. Remove all but 2 tablespoons of the bacon drippings from the skillet. Add the zucchini, onion and garlic to the skillet. Sauté for 3 minutes or until the vegetables are softened. Beat the eggs, salt, Italian seasoning and yogurt in a mixing bowl until well blended. Stir in the rice, cheese, zucchini mixture and crumbled bacon.

Pour the zucchini mixture into a buttered shallow 2-quart baking dish. Spread evenly in the dish. Bake at 350 degrees for 35 minutes or until the top is golden brown and the center is set. Let stand for 5 minutes before serving.

Yield: 6 servings

Apple Berry Breakfast Crisp

$^1/_4$ cup packed brown sugar
2 tablespoons flour
1 teaspoon cinnamon
4 cups thinly sliced, peeled apples
2 cups fresh or frozen blueberries or sliced strawberries
$^1/_4$ cup frozen orange juice concentrate, thawed
1 cup quick-cooking oats
$^1/_2$ cup packed brown sugar
2 tablespoons flour
$^1/_3$ cup butter or margarine, melted

Mix the $^1/_4$ cup brown sugar, 2 tablespoons flour and cinnamon in a small bowl. Combine the apples and blueberries in a large bowl. Add the orange juice concentrate and toss to coat. Add the brown sugar mixture and toss until the fruit is evenly coated. Spoon into an 8-inch square baking pan. Mix the oats, $^1/_2$ cup brown sugar, 2 tablespoons flour and melted butter in a bowl until crumbly. Sprinkle over the fruit. Bake at 350 degrees for 30 to 35 minutes or until the apples are tender. Serve warm with yogurt.

Yield: 9 servings

Cheese and Egg Casserole

3 cups seasoned croutons
15 eggs
2 cups milk
1 teaspoon salt
1 teaspoon pepper
$^3/_4$ teaspoon onion powder
2 tablespoons chopped fresh chives
1$^1/_2$ cups shredded Cheddar cheese

Arrange the croutons in a 9x13-inch baking dish coated with nonstick cooking spray or butter. Whisk the eggs, milk, salt, pepper, onion powder and chives in a bowl. Stir in the Cheddar cheese. Pour over the croutons in the baking dish. Cover and chill for 8 hours, stirring once during chilling. Uncover and stir. Bake at 350 degrees for 30 minutes or until set.

Yield: 8 to 10 servings

Three Sisters Frittata

1/4 cup olive oil
5 small yellow onions, thinly sliced
1 (14-ounce) can whole peeled tomatoes, chopped, drained
4 ounces smoked ham, prosciutto or pancetta, coarsely chopped
1/4 cup grated Parmesan cheese
1/2 teaspoon marjoram
1/4 teaspoon basil
1/4 teaspoon coarse salt
Large pinch of pepper
2 teaspoons finely chopped fresh parsley
2 tablespoons butter
6 eggs
Grated Parmesan cheese for garnish
Sliced fresh tomatoes seasoned with salt and pepper for garnish

Heat the olive oil in a medium skillet over medium-high heat. Add the onions and sauté for 6 to 8 minutes or until browned. Add the tomatoes and reduce the heat to medium. Sauté for 5 minutes. Remove the onions and tomatoes with a slotted spoon to a bowl and let cool. Add the smoked ham, Parmesan cheese, marjoram, basil, salt, pepper and parsley and mix lightly. Melt the butter in an ovenproof skillet over medium heat. Reduce the heat to very low when the foam subsides. Whisk the eggs in a small bowl. Stir into the tomato mixture. Pour into the skillet.

Cook, without stirring, over very low heat for 10 minutes. Shake the skillet gently once or twice during cooking. Place the skillet under a preheated broiler. Broil 4 inches from the heat source for 1 to 2 minutes or until set but not browned. Remove from the oven and invert onto a plate. Invert again onto a serving platter so that the top is up. Garnish with Parmesan cheese and seasoned tomatoes.

Yield: 6 servings

Port O'Call Omelet

1 pound bulk Italian sweet sausage
$1/2$ large onion, chopped
1 green bell pepper, chopped
5 potatoes, unpeeled, cubed
2 cups pasteurized egg substitute
Salt and pepper to taste
Salsa, sour cream and shredded Cheddar cheese

Cook the sausage in a nonstick Dutch oven until crumbly and cooked through; drain. Add the onion, bell pepper and potatoes to the Dutch oven and cover. Cook until the potatoes are tender but not mushy.

Stir in the sausage and egg substitute and cover. Cook over medium-low heat until the eggs are set. Season with salt and pepper.

Stir to fluff the omelette and serve with salsa, sour cream and shredded Cheddar cheese.

Yield: 6 servings

Sea Lion

We spotted the sea lion just offshore early in the morning while we sipped our coffee on the balcony. The sea lion watched us while we searched for sand crabs in the morning's outgoing tide, escorted us on our afternoon stroll along the beach, and bade us goodnight on our evening stroll. As magenta and crimson filled the western sky that evening, our new friend bobbed in the breakwaters just offshore.

Once again on the balcony, this time sipping the last of our pinot noir, we strained to see the sea lion in the blackness. Though we couldn't see him, we knew he was there, keeping watch over us and his home.

Dozens of covered bridges are scattered throughout the Willamette Valley, some still in use today.

Good Start Sandwiches

2 tablespoons butter or margarine
9 eggs
$1/2$ teaspoon salt
$1/4$ teaspoon pepper
4 ounces cream cheese, cut into cubes, softened
1 (12-ounce) can refrigerated biscuits
8 slices bacon, cooked, crumbled
1 cup shredded sharp Cheddar cheese

Melt the butter in a nonstick skillet. Whisk the eggs, salt and pepper in a bowl. Pour into the skillet and sprinkle with the cubes of cream cheese. Cook over medium heat until the eggs are set on the bottom. Draw a spatula through the eggs to make large curds. Cook until the eggs are thick but still moist. Remove from the heat and let cool.

Separate the biscuits and place on a lightly floured surface. Roll or pat each one to a 6-inch circle. Spoon the egg mixture onto the biscuits. Top with the crumbled bacon and Cheddar cheese. Brush the edges of the biscuits with water. Fold the biscuits over the filling and seal the edges. Arrange on a greased baking sheet. Bake at 375 degrees for 10 to 12 minutes.

Yield: 8 servings

Valley Sunrise Bacon Squares

1 teaspoon butter
1 (6-ounce) package Canadian bacon, cut into thin strips
$1/2$ cup shredded Swiss cheese
$1/4$ cup grated Parmesan cheese
2 tablespoons chopped fresh parsley
$2^1/2$ cups buttermilk baking mix
1 egg, beaten
1 cup milk
1 egg yolk, beaten

Melt the butter in a large skillet over medium heat. Add the Canadian bacon and sauté for 6 minutes. Remove from the heat and stir in the Swiss cheese, Parmesan cheese and parsley. Combine the baking mix, egg and milk in a bowl. Stir until well mixed. Spread half the dough in the bottom of a greased 8-inch square baking pan. Top with the cheese mixture. Spread with the remaining dough. Brush with the beaten egg yolk. Bake at 350 degrees for 25 to 30 minutes. Remove to a wire rack and let cool in the pan. Cut into squares when cool.

Yield: 12 squares

Crab Soufflé

6 slices white bread, crusts trimmed,
    cut into 1-inch squares
1 cup crab meat
$^{1}/_{2}$ cup chopped celery
$^{1}/_{4}$ cup chopped onion
$^{1}/_{4}$ cup mayonnaise
2 eggs
1$^{1}/_{2}$ cups milk
Salt and white pepper to taste
$^{1}/_{2}$ cup cream of mushroom soup
$^{3}/_{4}$ cup (about) shredded Cheddar cheese
Paprika to taste (optional)

Arrange half the bread squares in the bottom of a buttered round
baking dish. Mix the crab, celery, onion and mayonnaise in a
bowl. Spoon on top of the bread in the baking dish. Top with the
remaining bread squares.

Beat the eggs and milk in a bowl. Season with salt and pepper. Pour
over the bread mixture. Cover and chill overnight.

Bake, uncovered, at 325 degrees for 15 minutes. Spoon the soup
on top and sprinkle with the Cheddar cheese and paprika. Bake for
30 to 45 minutes longer.

Yield: 6 servings

Crab

*Only mature male crabs
measuring at least
6$^{1}/_{4}$ inches across the shell
may be harvested. Juvenile
males and all females are
returned live to the sea to
insure healthy stocks for future
harvests. A leg-sized male crab
is generally assumed to be
nearing 4 years of age, and
has shed his shell up to
16 times. —Oregon Crab
Commission*

*Oregon is the nation's leading producer of
Christmas trees, growing more than 8 million firs
for living rooms around the world.*

Spinach Soufflé

2 (10-ounce) packages frozen chopped spinach,
    thawed, well drained
1 (32-ounce) container small curd cottage cheese
6 eggs, beaten
8 ounces shredded sharp Cheddar cheese (Tillamook)
5 tablespoons flour
Salt and pepper to taste

Mix the spinach, cottage cheese, eggs, Cheddar cheese and flour in a bowl. Season with salt and pepper. Pour into a well-buttered 9-inch soufflé or deep baking dish. Bake at 350 degrees for 1 hour.

Yield: 6 servings

Apple Soup with Calvados

$1/2$ cup (1 stick) butter
1 onion, sliced
6 apples, peeled, cored, sliced
6 cups chicken stock
1 cinnamon stick
$1/4$ teaspoon nutmeg
Salt and pepper to taste
2 cups heavy cream
$1/2$ cup Calvados

Melt the butter in a large saucepan. Add the onion and apples and sauté until softened. Stir in the chicken stock, cinnamon stick and nutmeg. Season with salt and pepper. Simmer for 30 minutes. Remove the cinnamon stick and discard. Purée the soup in a blender in batches. Pour into a bowl and stir in the cream. Cover and chill. Stir in the Calvados and serve.

Yield: 6 servings

Chicken Salad Spread

4 cups finely chopped cooked chicken (about 6 large breasts)
24 ounces cream cheese, softened
3/4 cup chopped golden raisins
1/2 cup flaked coconut, toasted
4 ribs celery, finely chopped
6 green onions, finely chopped
1/4 cup slivered almonds, toasted, finely chopped
1 tablespoon curry powder
1/2 teaspoon salt
1/2 teaspoon pepper
1 tablespoon grated fresh gingerroot
Fresh parsley sprigs, sliced yellow squash and
    toasted almonds for garnish

Combine the chicken, cream cheese, raisins, coconut, celery, green onions, almonds, curry powder, salt, pepper and gingerroot in a large bowl. Stir until well mixed. Shape into a heart or star and place on a serving plate. Garnish with parsley sprigs, slices of squash and toasted almonds.

Yield: 12 to 15 servings

Northwest Espresso To Go

12 ounces semisweet chocolate
4 ounces unsweetened chocolate
3/4 cup heavy cream
3 tablespoons instant espresso powder
1/4 cup sugar
1/4 cup (1/2 stick) unsalted butter
30 individual chocolate-covered espresso beans

Chop the semisweet and unsweetened chocolate into 1/4-inch pieces. Place in a 4-quart heatproof bowl. Heat the cream, espresso powder, sugar and butter in a 1 1/2-quart saucepan over medium-high heat. Stir to dissolve the sugar when the mixture is hot. Bring to a boil. Pour over the chopped chocolate and let stand 5 minutes. Stir until smooth to make espresso ganache.

Arrange 30 foil candy cups on a baking sheet. Spoon 2 level tablespoons of ganache into each cup. Top each with a chocolate-covered espresso bean. Chill for 1 hour or until firm. Serve immediately or store in the refrigerator in a tightly sealed container.

Yield: 30 candy cups

Frozen Blended Coffee and Cream

1 cup strong cold coffee
1 cup crushed ice
3/4 cup nonfat coffee-flavored yogurt or coffee ice cream
2 tablespoons sugar

Combine the coffee, ice, yogurt and sugar in a blender container. Pulse for 20 to 30 seconds or until smooth.

Yield: 2 or 3 servings

Fruit Smoothie

2 ripe bananas, cut in half
3/4 to 1 cup plain yogurt
1/2 cup milk
1/2 cup orange juice
1 cup combination of frozen raspberries and strawberries (or other frozen fruit)
1/2 cup crushed ice
1/2 teaspoon vanilla extract
1 teaspoon honey

Purée the bananas, yogurt, milk, orange juice, frozen raspberries and strawberries, crushed ice, vanilla and honey in a blender until smooth. Serve at once.

Yield: 1 or 2 servings

Drive-Thru Coffee

Espresso, cappuccino, lattes, mochas, and overdrives. Skinny, fat, short, tall, iced, extra shots, whipped cream. This is the lingo of the drive-thru coffee stand. Scattered throughout our valley on various street corners and in parking lots, they brew wake-up calls from the wee morning hours until evening comes. Cars lineup four and five deep waiting for their morning pick-me-up.

Don't mind getting out of your car? There is fresh gourmet coffee available everywhere. Coffee beans are roasted locally here in Lane County, giving our java an exceptionally fresh aroma and taste. This isn't your Grandma's coffee anymore. We are now sophisticated in our coffee choices and we'll never go back to canned again.

Perfect Bloody Mary

1 (5-ounce) can V-8 picante vegetable juice, chilled
2 ounces Absolut vodka, chilled
Juice of $1/2$ lime
$1/4$ teaspoon prepared horseradish
Dash of Worcestershire sauce
2 dashes Tabasco sauce
1 Oregon Blue Lake spiced green bean
Lime wedge for garnish

Fill a shaker with ice. Add the vegetable juice, vodka, lime juice, horseradish, Worcestershire sauce and Tabasco sauce. Shake well. Pour into a 12-ounce glass. Add the bean and garnish with a lime wedge.

Yield: 1 serving

Bourbon Milk Punch

$1^1/2$ teaspoons pure vanilla extract
1 cup sugar
2 cups heavy cream
4 cups milk
1 cup plus 2 tablespoons bourbon
Freshly grated nutmeg for garnish

Whisk the vanilla and sugar in a large bowl. Whisk in the cream, milk and bourbon. Pour the punch into glass jars. Cover and chill for at least 2 hours. Serve cold in short 9-ounce glasses. Garnish with the grated nutmeg.

Note: The punch can be made up to 3 days ahead. Cover and chill.

Yield: 2 quarts

Let's Do Lunch!

Let's Do Lunch! offers a medley of salads, soups, sandwiches, and desserts, all with delectably fresh ingredients. Lunch can allude to mid-morning, noon, or mid-afternoon fare and can be casual, formal, indoor, outdoor, or even constitute a party or luncheon.

Having girlfriends and their kids over for a play date? How about serving a light meal everyone will enjoy, such as some variety of chicken salad, bread, and an easy-to-eat cookie bar for dessert. You're hosting a baby shower for sixteen? Combine a soup with two salads, bread, and a light dessert, and your luncheon is set. Tea sandwiches make an easy, fabulous appetizer. Weekends with the family also pose challenges for lunch. It seems everyone is hungry at different times. Instead of cooking at a set time, why not make a salad ahead of time and refrigerate so everyone can eat when hungry? Have a hearty soup on hand that can be quickly reheated, along with bread to satisfy a crowd of kids after a morning soccer game.

Lunch fare doesn't have to be complex to be delicious and satisfying. There is an abundance of ingredients sprinkled from the Coast to the Cascades to deliver incredible flavors to your lunch table, whether for a casual get-together or a more formal affair.

Clearwater Falls cascading past moss-covered rocks in Umpqua National Forest, Oregon

photo by Steve Terrill

Let's Do Lunch! Contents

Cottage Soup

$^{1}/_{4}$ cup dried black-eyed peas
$^{1}/_{4}$ cup dried butter beans or large lima beans
$^{1}/_{4}$ cup dried pinto beans
$^{1}/_{4}$ cup dried navy beans
$^{1}/_{4}$ cup dried small lima beans
$^{1}/_{4}$ cup dried red beans
$^{1}/_{4}$ cup dried great Northern beans
$^{1}/_{4}$ cup pearl barley
$^{1}/_{4}$ cup split green peas
$^{1}/_{4}$ cup dried lentils
8 ounces ham or ham hock
8 cups water
1 large onion, chopped
1 (29-ounce) can tomatoes
1 rib celery, chopped
1 teaspoon chili powder
$^{1}/_{2}$ garlic clove, minced, or $^{1}/_{4}$ teaspoon garlic powder
Salt and pepper to taste

Place the black-eyed peas, butter beans, pinto beans, navy beans, lima beans, red beans and great Northern beans in a colander and rinse well. Remove to a large saucepan. Add the barley, split peas, lentils and ham. Cover with the water.

Bring to a boil, stirring occasionally. Reduce the heat. Simmer for 2 to 2$^{1}/_{2}$ hours or until the beans are tender. Stir in the onion, tomatoes, celery, chili powder and garlic. Season with salt and pepper. Simmer for 30 minutes or until the vegetables are tender.

Yield: 12 to 15 servings

Leek Soup

2 pounds leeks
1/4 cup (1/2 stick) butter
5 cups chicken broth
2 potatoes, peeled, cut into small pieces
Salt and pepper to taste
Chopped chives for garnish

Rinse the leeks well. Remove the green portion and discard. Cut the white portion into thin slices. Melt the butter in a large saucepan. Add the sliced leeks and sauté for about 4 minutes. Stir in the broth and potatoes and bring to a boil. Reduce the heat to medium-low and cover. Cook for 15 minutes or until the potatoes are tender. Season with salt and pepper. Ladle into warmed bowls and garnish with the chopped chives.

Yield: 6 to 8 servings

Greek Lemon Chicken Soup

8 cups chicken broth
3/4 cup orzo
1 boneless skinless chicken breast, cut into 1/4-inch slices
3 eggs
1/3 cup fresh lemon juice
Salt and pepper to taste
2 tablespoons chopped fresh flat-leaf parsley for garnish

Bring the chicken broth to a boil in a large saucepan over medium-high heat. Reduce the heat to medium and stir in the orzo. Cook, uncovered, for 15 minutes. Add the chicken. Cook for 5 minutes.

Whisk the eggs in a bowl. Add the lemon juice gradually. Whisk in about 1/2 cup of the hot soup into the egg mixture. Reduce the heat to very low under the soup. Whisk the egg mixture slowly into the hot soup to thicken the soup slightly. Season with salt and pepper. Ladle the soup into bowls and garnish with the parsley.

Yield: 6 to 8 servings

Cranberry, Pear and Walnut Mesclun Salad

Caramelized Walnuts
1 cup sugar
$^{1}/_{3}$ cup water
1 tablespoon butter
1 teaspoon cinnamon
$^{1}/_{4}$ teaspoon cream of tartar
2 cups walnut halves

Cranberry Vinaigrette
$^{1}/_{4}$ cup frozen cranberry juice cocktail concentrate, thawed
$^{1}/_{4}$ cup white wine vinegar
2 teaspoons Dijon mustard
$^{1}/_{4}$ teaspoon salt
Freshly ground pepper to taste
$^{1}/_{2}$ cup vegetable oil

Salad
8 cups mesclun greens
$^{1}/_{2}$ cup dried cranberries
$^{1}/_{2}$ red onion, thinly sliced
1 red pear, cored, thinly sliced

For the walnuts, combine the sugar and water in a saucepan over medium heat. Bring to a boil, stirring until the sugar dissolves. Cook until threads form or until a candy thermometer registers 230 degrees. Add the butter, cinnamon, cream of tartar and walnuts. Stir until the nuts are well coated. Spread the nuts on a plate or waxed paper to dry.

For the vinaigrette, mix the cranberry cocktail concentrate, vinegar, mustard and salt in a bowl. Season with pepper. Whisk in the oil gradually. Cover and chill until ready to use.

For the salad, place the mesclun and cranberries in a large bowl. Toss with enough Cranberry Vinaigrette to moisten. Divide between 6 salad plates. Arrange the red onion and pear on the salads. Top with the Caramelized Walnuts.

Yield: 6 servings

Romaine Salad with Mustard Dressing

Waterfall

As I hiked along the mossy bank of the river, a faint roar of rushing water broke the silence of the forest. When I finally reached the cascade, the roar was deafening. A 120-foot plume of water plunged into a deep swimming hole, gracefully fanned over a rim of rock, pummeled through a cluster of massive boulders, and continued its race through the narrow chasm. I was humbled and awed by the majesty of yet another Cascade Range waterfall.

Mustard Dressing
1¹/2 teaspoons prepared yellow mustard
3 tablespoons cider vinegar
3 tablespoons sugar
3 hard-cooked egg yolks, chopped

Salad
4 slices bacon
16 ounces romaine, rinsed, dried, torn into bite-size pieces
2 green onions, chopped
3 hard-cooked egg whites, chopped

For the dressing, whisk the mustard, vinegar, sugar and egg yolks in a bowl. Cover and chill until ready to use.

For the salad, cook the bacon in a skillet until crisp. Remove with a slotted spoon to paper towels to drain. Crumble when cool. Reserve 1/3 cup bacon drippings and keep warm.

Place the romaine in a salad bowl. Add the Mustard Dressing and toss to coat. Add the bacon drippings and toss again. Top with the crumbled bacon, green onions and egg whites.

Yield: 6 servings

Curried Spinach Salad

Curry Dressing
2/3 cup canola oil
1/4 cup garlic wine vinegar
2 teaspoons white wine such as sauterne (optional)
2 teaspoons soy sauce
1 teaspoon sugar
1 teaspoon dry mustard
1/2 teaspoon curry powder
1/2 teaspoon salt
1/2 teaspoon seasoned pepper

Salad
2 bunches fresh spinach leaves, rinsed well, dried,
   torn into bite-size pieces
5 slices bacon, cooked crisp, drained, crumbled
2 hard-cooked eggs, finely chopped
10 to 12 mushrooms, thinly sliced
1/2 Bermuda onion, thinly sliced (optional)

For the dressing, combine the oil, wine vinegar, white wine, soy sauce, sugar, dry mustard, curry powder, salt and pepper in a jar with a tight-fitting lid. Cover the jar and shake to mix.

For the salad, toss the spinach, bacon, eggs, mushrooms and onion in a large bowl. Pour the Curry Dressing over the greens and toss to coat. Serve immediately.

Yield: 6 servings

Asian Chicken Salad

Wallowa Mountains

Outside of Joseph, the Wallowa Mountains offer an incredible opportunity for enjoying the Eastern Oregon experience with horseback trail riding, especially in the summer months. Often called the "Little Alps," this area amazes even the most well traveled Oregonian. Green grassy hills are dotted with colorful wildflowers, and in the distance, the jagged snow-capped mountains against the blue sky command attention.

The pungent smell of the campfire draws you back to camp, just in time to see steaks and vegetables being thrown on the grill. As you enjoy your meal and the tranquility of the setting, you once again realize there is nothing better than Oregon's great outdoors.

Salad
4 whole boneless skinless chicken breasts
2 tablespoons hoisin sauce
2 tablespoons black bean paste
2 tablespoons soy sauce
2 tablespoons sugar
2 tablespoons minced garlic
1 head iceberg lettuce, chopped
1 small bunch green onions, chopped
1½ to 2 cups roasted cashews, chopped
1 bunch cilantro, finely chopped
2 (3-ounce) packages ramen noodles, crumbled

Hoisin Dressing
2 tablespoons vegetable oil
2 tablespoons sesame oil
2 tablespoons hoisin sauce
2 tablespoons sugar
2 tablespoons minced garlic
1 teaspoon chile oil

For the salad, arrange the chicken in a shallow baking dish. Mix the hoisin sauce, black bean paste, soy sauce, sugar and garlic in a bowl. Pour over the chicken. Cover and chill for 8 hours.

Bake the chicken, uncovered, in the marinade at 350 degrees for 30 minutes or until cooked through. Shred the chicken when cool.

Mix the lettuce, green onions, cashews, cilantro, crumbled noodles and shredded chicken in a salad bowl.

For the dressing, whisk the vegetable oil, sesame oil, hoisin sauce, sugar, garlic and chile oil in a small bowl. Add to the salad and toss to mix. Cover and chill. Serve chilled.

Yield: 4 to 8 servings

Chicken, Cashew and Grape Salad

6 boneless skinless chicken breasts, cooked, cubed
2 cups red seedless grapes, halved
2 cups salted cashew halves
2 ribs celery, sliced
3/4 cup (or more) mayonnaise-type salad dressing
1/2 cup sour cream
1 tablespoon tarragon or white wine vinegar

Mix the chicken, grapes, cashews and celery in a large bowl. Mix the salad dressing, sour cream and vinegar in a small bowl. Add to the chicken mixture and toss to coat. Chill for at least 1 hour before serving.

Yield: 7 or 8 servings

Crunchy Chinese Chicken Salad

Salad
2 heads Chinese cabbage, chopped
1 bunch green onions, chopped
5 boneless skinless chicken breasts, cooked, cut into bite-size pieces
1 (2-ounce) package sliced almonds
2 (3-ounce) packages oriental-flavor ramen noodles, crumbled
Sunflower kernels

Dressing
2/3 cup seasoned rice vinegar
2/3 cup salad oil
6 tablespoons sugar, or to taste
1 package oriental-flavor ramen noodle seasoning

For the salad, combine the cabbage, green onions, chicken, almonds and noodles in a bowl and mix well. Sprinkle the sunflower kernels over the top.

For the dressing, whisk the rice vinegar, oil, sugar and seasoning in a small bowl. Add to the salad and toss to mix. Serve immediately.

Yield: 6 to 8 servings

Chop Chop Salad

Italian Vinaigrette
1 egg yolk
1 tablespoon water
1 tablespoon Dijon mustard
2 tablespoons minced garlic
1/2 teaspoon salt
1 teaspoon coarsely ground
  pepper
1/2 teaspoon dry mustard
2 teaspoons oregano
1/2 teaspoon sugar
1/3 cup red wine vinegar
2 tablespoons lemon juice
1 cup olive oil

Salad
1/2 cup cooked chick peas
1 head iceberg lettuce, chopped
  into 1/4 to 1/2-inch pieces
1 cup fresh basil leaves, chopped
1 cup shredded mozzarella cheese
2 cups chopped cooked chicken
8 ounces dry wine salami,
  chopped
8 ounces plum tomatoes, chopped
1/2 cup shredded provolone cheese
3 thin green onions, thinly sliced
8 lettuce leaves

For the vinaigrette, whisk the egg yolk and water in a small microwave-safe bowl. Cover with a microwave-safe plate. Heat on High for 10 seconds or until the mixture starts to expand. Heat on High for 5 seconds. Whisk and heat on High for 5 more seconds. Whisk and cover with the plate. Let stand for 1 minute. Place the egg, Dijon mustard, garlic, salt, pepper, dry mustard, oregano, sugar, wine vinegar and lemon juice in a food processor container. Process until mixed. Add the olive oil in a slow stream, processing until emulsified.

For the salad, combine the chick peas, chopped lettuce, basil, mozzarella cheese, chicken, salami, half the tomatoes, half the provolone cheese and half the green onions in a bowl. Add enough of the vinaigrette to coat and toss to mix. Divide between 8 lettuce-lined salad plates. Garnish with the remaining tomatoes, provolone cheese and green onions.

Note: Pour any remaining vinaigrette into a jar with a tight-fitting lid. Seal and chill and reserve for another use.

Yield: 8 servings

Italian-Style Pasta Salad

6 ounces spaghetti or vermicelli
1 (6-ounce) jar marinated artichoke hearts
$1/2$ small zucchini, sliced
1 carrot, peeled, shredded
2 ounces salami, cut into strips
1 cup shredded mozzarella cheese
2 tablespoons grated Parmesan cheese
1 ($2^1/4$-ounce) can sliced olives (about $1/2$ cup)
2 tablespoons vegetable oil
2 tablespoons white wine vinegar
$3/4$ teaspoon dry mustard
$1/2$ teaspoon oregano
$1/2$ teaspoon basil
1 garlic clove, minced

Break the pasta in half. Cook in boiling salted water in a saucepan until tender; drain well. Drain the artichokes and reserve the marinade. Chop the artichokes coarsely. Cut the zucchini slices in half.

Combine the drained pasta, artichokes, zucchini, carrot, salami, mozzarella cheese, Parmesan cheese and olives in a large bowl. Whisk the reserved artichoke marinade, oil, wine vinegar, dry mustard, oregano, basil and garlic in a small bowl. Pour over the pasta mixture and toss to coat. Cover and chill for several hours before serving.

Yield: 6 servings

Rice and Shrimp Salad

2 (7-ounce) packages herb and butter-flavored rice mix
2 (6-ounce) jars marinated artichokes
3/4 pound small shrimp, cooked, peeled, deveined
1 green bell pepper, chopped
1 bunch green onions, chopped
12 pitted green olives, sliced
1/2 cup mayonnaise
1 teaspoon curry powder

Cook the rice mix according to package directions. Remove to a bowl and let cool. Cover and chill overnight.

Drain the artichokes and reserve the marinade from 1 of the jars. Chop the artichokes finely. Combine the chilled rice, artichokes, shrimp, bell pepper, green onions and olives in a large bowl.

Mix the mayonnaise, curry powder and reserved artichoke marinade in a small bowl. Add to the rice mixture. Toss to mix well.

Yield: 6 to 8 servings

Stunning views of the 10,000 feet Three Sisters Mountains grace Tokatee Golf Course on the McKenzie River.

Cucumber Tea Sandwiches

8 ounces cream cheese, softened
1/3 cup mayonnaise
1 medium cucumber, peeled, seeded, chopped
1/4 teaspoon salt
1 teaspoon chopped fresh dill
20 slices sandwich bread
Fresh strawberries or fresh dill sprigs for garnish (optional)

Process the cream cheese and mayonnaise in a food processor until smooth. Add the cucumber, salt and dill. Process for 15 seconds. Spread the cucumber mixture on 10 slices of bread. Top with the remaining bread. Trim the crusts and cut diagonally into triangles. Arrange on a serving platter and cover with plastic wrap. Chill until ready to serve. Cut the strawberries in half, leaving the stem attached. Arrange the strawberry halves or dill sprigs around the sandwiches and serve.

Yield: 20 servings

Chicken Salad Tea Sandwiches

1 1/2 cups (about) mayonnaise
1/4 teaspoon salt
1/2 teaspoon celery salt
1/4 teaspoon pepper
2 teaspoons tarragon
3 shallots, minced
3 boneless skinless chicken breasts, cooked, shredded
12 slices sandwich bread, crusts trimmed
1/2 cup finely chopped smoked almonds

Mix the 1 cup of the mayonnaise, salt, celery salt, pepper, tarragon and shallots in a bowl. Add the cooked chicken and stir to mix. Spread 1 tablespoon of the remaining mayonnaise on each of 6 slices of the bread. Spread the chicken salad on the other 6 slices. Put the bread together to make sandwich. Spread a small amount of mayonnaise around the edge of each sandwich. Press the chopped almonds into the mayonnaise. Cut the sandwiches into triangles and serve.

Yield: 8 servings

Smoked Turkey Focaccia Sandwiches with Fresh Herbs

Davis Lake

We paddled our canoe to the center of Davis Lake for an unobstructed view of the Three Sisters. The calm water reflected the brilliant snowcapped mountains. Two hawks circled above the meadow by the lake. We unpacked our picnic lunch of cheese and crackers and blackberries and popped our bottle of pinot gris. The blackberries from the morning's forage were so juicy we had to rinse our hands frequently in the lake.

The heat of the August sun on our skin made the soft splash welcome and refreshing. Soon we were dangling our bare toes in the cool crisp water and rippling the pristine reflection. We lingered a long time, not wanting to end such a peaceful afternoon.

1 (8- to 9-inch round, 1^1/$_2$-inch thick) loaf focaccia
8 ounces cream cheese, softened
2 to 3 tablespoons milk
^{1}/$_4$ cup oil-pack sun-dried tomatoes, drained, chopped
4 teaspoons chopped fresh basil leaves
4 teaspoons chopped fresh thyme
1 small garlic clove, minced
1^1/$_2$ cups packed fresh spinach leaves, rinsed well, drained, dried
8 ounces thinly sliced smoked deli turkey

Cut the focaccia in half horizontally with a serrated knife. Arrange the 2 halves cut side up on a work surface.

Mix the cream cheese and milk in a small bowl until smooth. Add the sun-dried tomatoes, basil, thyme and garlic and mix well. Spread ^{1}/$_4$ of the cream cheese mixture to the edge of each focaccia round.

Layer the spinach and turkey on top. Spread with the remaining cream cheese. Wrap each round individually in plastic wrap. Chill for at least 1 hour or up to 12 hours. Cut each round into 8 wedges and serve.

Note: You may cut each round into 5 strips and cut each strip into 1^1/$_2$-inch pieces to make 48 appetizer portions.

Yield: 8 servings

Dungeness Hot Crab Sandwiches

1 cup cooked Dungeness crab meat
1 (4¹/4-ounce) can chopped black olives
1¹/2 cups shredded Swiss cheese
3 green onions, finely chopped
¹/3 cup mayonnaise
Salt and pepper to taste
8 kaiser rolls, halved crosswise

Mix the crab meat, black olives, Swiss cheese, green onions and mayonnaise in a bowl. Season with salt and pepper. Spread the mixture evenly on the rolls. Wrap each roll in foil and place on a baking sheet. Bake at 375 degrees for 20 minutes.

Yield: 8 servings

Savory Carrots with Hazelnuts

4 large carrots, peeled
¹/4 cup (¹/2 stick) butter or margarine
2 tablespoons honey
¹/4 teaspoon nutmeg
¹/2 teaspoon salt
¹/4 teaspoon pepper
3 tablespoons finely chopped fresh parsley
1 tablespoon apple juice
¹/4 cup toasted hazelnuts
¹/4 teaspoon garlic powder

Steam the carrots until tender-crisp. Remove to a plate and let cool enough to handle. Grate the carrots into a bowl and set aside. Melt the butter in a saucepan over medium-low heat. Stir in the honey, nutmeg, salt, pepper, parsley, apple juice, hazelnuts and garlic powder. Add the grated carrots and sauté until just heated through.

Yield: 6 servings

Fresh Green Bean and Tomato Platter

Dressing
1 tablespoon lemon juice
1 tablespoon white wine vinegar
1 teaspoon Dijon mustard
1/2 teaspoon dried basil, crumbled
1/2 teaspoon sugar
Salt and pepper to taste
1/3 cup olive oil

Salad
1 1/2 pounds fresh green beans, trimmed
1/2 cup crumbled feta cheese
1/2 cup finely chopped Bermuda onion
4 to 5 Roma tomatoes, cored, chopped
4 to 5 large fresh basil leaves

For the dressing, combine the lemon juice, wine vinegar, mustard, basil and sugar in a bowl or jar with a tight-fitting lid. Season with salt and pepper. Add the oil and shake or whisk until thickened.

For the salad, cook the beans in rapidly boiling water in a saucepan for 3 to 5 minutes or until tender-crisp. Plunge the beans into ice water in a bowl. Drain and pat dry with paper towels when cool. Arrange the beans on a serving platter. Drizzle the dressing over the beans. Top with the feta cheese and chopped onion. Arrange the chopped tomatoes around the edge of the beans. Slice the basil leaves thinly and sprinkle over the top.

Yield: 8 servings

Grilled Summer Squash with Parmesan Basil Dressing

Grilled Squash
4 medium-large zucchini, trimmed, halved lengthwise
4 medium-large yellow crookneck squash, trimmed,
    halved lengthwise
2 tablespoons olive oil
Salt and pepper to taste

Parmesan Basil Dressing
$1/2$ cup chopped fresh basil leaves
$1/3$ cup freshly grated Parmesan cheese (about 1 ounce)
2 tablespoons balsamic vinegar
2 tablespoons olive oil
Salt and pepper to taste

For the squash, prepare the grill to cook at medium heat. Place the squash on a large baking sheet. Brush all over with the olive oil. Season with salt and pepper. Place the squash on the grill and cook for 10 minutes or until tender and lightly browned. Turn the squash occasionally while grilling. Remove to a plate and let cool. Cut the squash diagonally into 1-inch slices and place in a large bowl.

For the dressing, combine the basil, Parmesan cheese, balsamic vinegar and olive oil in a bowl and mix well. Add to the squash and toss to mix. Season with salt and pepper and serve.

Yield: 6 servings

Italian-Style Marinated Tomatoes

4 large tomatoes
6 tablespoons finely chopped fresh parsley
1 garlic clove, minced
6 tablespoons olive oil
2 tablespoons cider vinegar
1 teaspoon salt
1/2 teaspoon basil
1/8 teaspoon freshly ground pepper

Place the tomatoes in a saucepan of boiling water for 1 minute or until the skins split. Plunge the tomatoes into ice water in a bowl. Remove from the water and drain. Slip off the skins and core.

Cut the tomatoes into 1/4-inch-thick slices. Arrange a single layer of tomato slices in a bowl or baking dish. Sprinkle with some of the parsley. Add another layer of tomatoes and parsley. Repeat the layers until all the tomatoes and parsley have been used.

Whisk the garlic, olive oil, vinegar, salt, basil and pepper in a bowl. Pour over the tomatoes and parsley. Cover and chill for at least 3 hours or overnight. Baste the tomatoes occasionally with the marinade while chilling.

Yield: 4 to 6 servings

Oregon leads the nation in peppermint, Christmas tree, grass seed, blackberry, raspberry and hazelnut production.

Two-Minute Chocolate Mousse

1 cup chocolate chips
2 eggs
3 tablespoons coffee or chocolate liqueur
3/4 cup scalded milk
Whipped cream or nondairy whipped topping

Set aside 1 tablespoon of the chocolate chips. Combine the remaining chocolate chips, eggs and liqueur in a mixing bowl. Beat for 20 seconds. Add the hot milk and beat for 2 minutes or until the chocolate is melted and the mixture is smooth. Pour into dessert bowls or stemmed glasses. Chill completely. Garnish with the whipped cream and reserved chocolate chips.

Note: If you prefer not to use raw eggs, use an equivalent amount of pasteurized egg substitute.

Yield: 4 servings

Hungarian Poppy Seed Cookies

1 cup (2 sticks) butter, softened
1 cup sugar
1 egg
1 teaspoon vanilla extract
1/2 teaspoon cinnamon
1 1/2 cups finely chopped almonds
1/2 cup poppy seeds
2 cups sifted flour
1/4 teaspoon salt
2 tablespoons sugar

Beat the butter and 1 cup sugar in a mixing bowl until light and fluffy. Add the egg, vanilla and cinnamon and beat for 2 minutes. Add the almonds and poppy seeds and beat for 2 minutes. Stir in the flour and salt gradually. Cover and chill for 2 to 3 hours or until the dough is stiff enough to handle. Shape the dough into 2-inch diameter rolls. Coat the rolls with 2 tablespoons sugar. Wrap in waxed paper and chill overnight.

Cut the rolls into thin slices and place on an ungreased cookie sheet. Bake at 325 degrees for 12 to 15 minutes or until the cookies start to brown. Remove to a wire rack to cool. Store the cooled cookies in an airtight container.

Yield: 6 dozen cookies

Lemon Love Notes Bar Cookies

Bar Cookies
3/4 cup (1 1/2 sticks) butter, softened
1 1/2 cups flour
6 tablespoons confectioners' sugar
3 tablespoons fresh lemon juice
3 tablespoons flour
3 eggs, beaten
3/4 teaspoon baking powder
1 1/2 cups sugar

Frosting
1 cup plus 2 tablespoons confectioners' sugar
3/4 teaspoon vanilla extract
1 1/2 tablespoons butter, softened
2 1/4 teaspoons (or more) milk

For the cookies, combine the butter, 1 1/2 cups flour and confectioners' sugar in a bowl. Stir until blended. Pat into a 9x13-inch baking pan. Bake at 350 degrees for 15 minutes. Remove to a wire rack to cool.

Stir the lemon juice, 3 tablespoons flour, eggs, baking powder and sugar in a bowl until well mixed. Pour over the baked crust. Bake at 350 degrees for 25 minutes. Remove to a wire rack to cool.

For the frosting, beat the confectioners' sugar, vanilla, butter and milk in a mixing bowl to a smooth spreading consistency. Add more milk if necessary. Spread over the cooled filling. Cut into bars.

Yield: 4 dozen bars

Oatmeal Jumbles

1/2 cup (1 stick) margarine, softened
3/4 cup sugar
3/4 cup packed brown sugar
1 egg
1 1/2 teaspoons vanilla extract
1 1/4 cups flour
1/2 teaspoon baking soda
1/2 teaspoon baking powder
3/4 cup rolled oats
3/4 cup granola
3/4 cup flaked coconut
1 cup chocolate chips

Beat the margarine, sugar, brown sugar, egg and vanilla in a mixing bowl at medium speed until light and fluffy. Mix the flour, baking soda, baking powder, oats, granola, coconut and chocolate chips in a bowl. Beat the dry ingredients into the sugar mixture gradually. Beat until well mixed.

Form the dough into 1-inch balls and place 2 inches apart on a cookie sheet. Bake at 350 degrees for 12 to 15 minutes or until just the bottom of the cookies are golden brown. Remove to a wire rack to cool.

Note: You may substitute an additional 3/4 cup rolled oats in place of the coconut, if desired.

Yield: 3 dozen cookies

Coffee

Coffee was the main beverage on the Oregon Trail. The pioneers boiled water and coffee in a kettle on the campfire. To help the grounds settle and reduce sediment, broken eggshells were dumped into the kettle. When pouring, most of the grounds and sediment would then stick to the filmy side of the eggshells.

Coffee remains a favorite beverage of Oregonians and our Pacific Northwest neighbors. Today, however, most Oregonians prefer coffee brewed or pressed and without eggshells.

Coffee kiosks and drive-thrus can be found in almost every town and every few blocks in the cities. A kiosk at a viewpoint of Highway 101 on the central Oregon coast is a perfect spot to stop and marvel at the Pacific splendor and sip a hazelnut latte.

Rocky Road Fudge Bars

Crust

$^{1}/_{2}$ cup (1 stick) butter or
    margarine
1 ounce unsweetened chocolate
1 cup sugar
1 cup flour
$^{1}/_{2}$ cup chopped nuts (optional)
1 teaspoon baking powder
1 teaspoon vanilla extract
2 eggs

Filling

6 ounces cream cheese, softened
$^{1}/_{4}$ cup ($^{1}/_{2}$ stick) butter or
    margarine, softened
$^{1}/_{2}$ cup sugar
2 tablespoons flour
1 egg
$^{1}/_{2}$ teaspoon vanilla extract
$^{1}/_{2}$ cup chopped nuts (optional)
1 cup chocolate chips
2 cups miniature marshmallows

Topping

$^{1}/_{4}$ cup ($^{1}/_{2}$ stick) butter or
    margarine
1 ounce unsweetened chocolate
2 ounces cream cheese, softened
$^{1}/_{4}$ cup milk
3 cups confectioners' sugar
1 teaspoon vanilla extract

For the crust, melt the butter and chocolate in a saucepan over low heat. Remove from the heat and add the sugar, flour, nuts, baking powder, vanilla and eggs. Stir until well mixed. Spread in the bottom of a greased 9x13-inch baking pan.

For the filling, beat the cream cheese, butter, sugar, flour, egg and vanilla in a mixing bowl until smooth. Stir in the nuts. Spread over the crust and sprinkle with the chocolate chips. Bake at 350 degrees for 25 to 30 minutes or until a wooden pick inserted in the center comes out clean. Sprinkle with the marshmallows and return to the oven. Bake for 2 minutes. Remove to a wire rack.

For the topping, melt the butter, chocolate and cream cheese in a large saucepan over low heat. Add the milk and stir until smooth. Add the confectioners' sugar and vanilla. Beat until smooth. Pour over the hot marshmallow filling and swirl with a knife. Let cool and cut into squares. Chill until ready to serve.

Yield: 4 dozen bars

White Chocolate Drops

16 ounces white chocolate, chopped
1/2 cup creamy peanut butter
11/2 cups crisp rice cereal
11/2 cups miniature marshmallows
1 cup unsalted dry-roasted peanuts
1/2 cup chocolate chips

Combine the white chocolate and peanut butter in a large heavy saucepan over low heat. Cook, stirring constantly, for 5 to 6 minutes or until smooth. Remove from the heat and stir in the rice cereal, marshmallows and peanuts.

Drop by rounded spoonfuls onto a plastic wrap- or waxed paper-lined baking sheet. Chill for 10 minutes or until set.

Place the chocolate chips in a small heavy plastic sealable bag. Submerge the sealed bag in hot water until the chocolate is melted.

Cut a tiny hole in one corner of the bag and drizzle the chocolate over the candies. Chill for 10 minutes. Store the candies in an airtight container.

Yield: about 2 dozen candies

Crater Lake

The late spring sunshine warmed the day and began to melt the heavy snowpack at Crater Lake. The cross-country ski around Rim Drive was silent except for the dripping snowmelt. At the scenic overlooks, the blinding white snow contrasted brilliantly with the clear sky and deep cobalt lake, the bluest blue imaginable.

Chipmunks joined us at some of the overlooks, very much interested in our trail mix. Realizing their winter food supply had probably been depleted by now, we shared our nuts with the forest critters.

Wagon train members who used them as landmarks first called the Three Sisters Mountains in the Cascade Range: Faith, Hope and Charity.

Weeknight Dinners

As Oregonians, we spend time in our great outdoors enjoying activities ranging from golfing and fishing to snow skiing and camping. We happily cheer on our children from the sidelines of the sport fields in rain or sun. We delight in sharing casual and relaxing meals with our family, friends, and neighbors. It is important to us to fill our families with healthy, nutritious, and savory foods.

Fortunately, stirring the taste buds does not have to be complicated. The fresh ingredients available here in the Willamette Valley allow us to prepare dinners that are quick, easy, and delicious. Coming home from a day on the slopes to the pungent aroma of a turkey breast roasting in the oven accompanied with Broccoli Bake and Scalloped Potato Casserole gives your family a sense of well-being and comfort as they walk in the door. In the summer months, after a day playing in the sunshine with your family and working up an appetite, take pleasure in eating delectable Roasted Chicken paired with Zucchini Stir-Fry with Garlic and Lime and Oregon Berry Cobbler in a relaxed outdoor setting.

These quick and easy weeknight dinner recipes are about bringing family and friends together to share not just the wonderful food, but the company and conversation that comes from enjoying a meal together.

Afternoon sun shines on Wizard Island reflecting on Crater Lake viewed in Crater Lake National Park, Oregon

photo by Steve Terrill

Weeknight Dinners
Contents

Weeknight Dinners *Menus*

Week 1

Night 1

Packaged salad greens
185   Basic Gourmet Salad Dressing
66   Tex-Mex Pie
73   Zucchini Stir-Fry with Garlic and Lime
76   Fresh Fruit Tart

Night 2

62   Papaya with Shrimp and Pomegranate
69   Sautéed Scallops with Lime
     Crusty hot French bread
75   Peanut Butter Pie

Night 3

61   Cucumber and Onion Salad
60   Corn Chowder
     Crisp crackers
77   Mixed Nut Squares

Night 4

62   Mozzarella, Tomato and Basil Salad
63   Quick and Easy Focaccia
64   Baked Ziti
     Spumanti ice cream

Night 5

Packaged salad greens
Salad dressing
68   Roasted Chicken
     Crusty hot French bread
69   Broccoli Bake
70   Glazed Carrots with Pecans
     Cookies
     Hot cappuccino

Weeknight Dinners *Menus*

Week 2

Night 1

Packaged salad greens topped with
crushed orange bits and roasted nuts
Salad dressing

67	Baked Chicken Dijon
72	Herbed Rice
70	Colonial Green Beans and Bacon

Fresh fruit

Night 2

Packaged salad greens

187	Basic Gourmet Salad Dressing
65	Herb-Stuffed Meat Pie

Refrigerated crescent rolls

75	Gingersnap Pears

Night 3

60	Cabbage Patch Soup

Crisp crackers

74	Oregon Berry Cobbler

Night 4

61	Berry Summer Salad
63	Tamale Casserole

Fresh fruit with ice cream

Night 5

Packaged salad greens with avocado and
hard-cooked egg slices
Salad dressing

68	Easy Aromatic Turkey
72	Scalloped Potato Casserole
70	Fresh Green Beans with Country Almond Butter

Coffee made from freshly ground decaffeinated coffee beans
Hazelnut biscotti dipped in melted chocolate

Cream of Broccoli Soup

1 1/2 pounds fresh broccoli
2 tablespoons butter
1 onion, finely chopped
1/4 cup flour
5 cups warm chicken broth
1 tablespoon lemon juice
2 cups milk
8 ounces Cheddar cheese, shredded
Salt and pepper to taste
2 tablespoons chopped parsley

Trim and coarsely chop the broccoli. Heat the butter in a large saucepan over medium-low heat until melted. Add the onion. Sauté for 5 to 7 minutes or until light brown. Sprinkle the flour over the onion. Cook for 1 minute, stirring constantly. Pour in the broth slowly, stirring constantly. Add the broccoli and lemon juice. Bring to a boil. Reduce the heat to low. Cook, covered, for 20 minutes or until the broccoli is tender.

Purée the soup in a food processor or blender in batches. Pour the puréed soup into a saucepan. Stir in the milk. Cook over low heat until heated through; do not boil.

Sprinkle the cheese over the soup. Cook until the cheese is melted, stirring constantly. Season with salt and pepper. Ladle into warm soup bowls. Garnish with parsley.

Yield: 6 to 8 servings

Cabbage Patch Soup

1 pound ground beef
1 small head green cabbage, chopped
2 large bell peppers, chopped
2 large onions, chopped
3 ribs celery, chopped
2 tablespoons chili powder
3 ripe tomatoes, chopped
3/4 cup (or more) water
Salt and pepper to taste

Brown the ground beef in a large saucepan over medium heat; drain. Stir in the cabbage, bell peppers, onions, celery, chili powder and tomatoes. Add the water to cover all ingredients. Season with salt and pepper. Cover and cook until the vegetables are tender.

Yield: 6 servings

Corn Chowder

2 tablespoons butter or margarine
1 cup chopped onion
1/2 cup chopped celery
1 1/2 cups diced, peeled potatoes
2 cups fresh or frozen corn kernels
1 teaspoon salt
1/4 teaspoon pepper
1 1/2 cups water
2 chicken bouillon cubes
1/4 teaspoon dried thyme,
    or 3/4 teaspoon chopped fresh thyme
2 cups milk
1 cup light cream

Melt the butter in a large saucepan over medium heat. Stir in the onion and celery and cook until the vegetables are softened. Add the potatoes, corn, salt, pepper, water, bouillon and thyme. Cover and simmer for 15 minutes or until the potatoes are tender. Stir in the milk and cream. Cook until heated through. Ladle into bowls and serve.

Yield: 4 servings

Berry Summer Salad

2 bunches fresh spinach leaves, rinsed well, dried, torn
2 pints fresh strawberries, hulled, halved
$1/2$ cup vegetable oil
$1/3$ cup sugar
$1/4$ cup cider vinegar
2 tablespoons sesame seeds
1 tablespoon poppy seeds
$1^{1}/2$ teaspoons minced onion
$1/4$ teaspoon Worcestershire sauce
$1/4$ teaspoon paprika

Place the spinach in a large bowl and top with the strawberries. Do not mix. Combine the oil, sugar, vinegar, sesame seeds, poppy seeds, onion, Worcestershire sauce and paprika in a blender or food processor container. Process until well combined and thickened, but do not overmix. Toss the dressing with the spinach and strawberries just before serving.

Note: You may substitute fresh raspberries in place of the strawberries.

Yield: 6 to 8 servings

Cucumber and Onion Salad

$1/2$ cup sour cream
2 tablespoons sugar
2 tablespoons vinegar
$1/2$ teaspoon salt
$1/4$ teaspoon freshly ground pepper
2 cups thinly sliced, peeled cucumbers
$1/2$ small onion, thinly sliced, separated into rings

Mix the sour cream, sugar, vinegar, salt and pepper in a medium bowl. Place the cucumbers and onion in a serving bowl. Add the sour cream mixture and toss to coat. Cover and chill. Serve chilled.

Yield: 4 servings

Mozzarella, Tomato and Basil Salad

3 ripe tomatoes, cored, sliced
12 ounces fresh mozzarella cheese, sliced
1 bunch fresh basil leaves
1/2 cup extra-virgin olive oil
1 tablespoon lemon juice or balsamic vinegar
Salt and pepper to taste

Arrange the tomato slices and mozzarella slices alternately on a serving platter. Tuck the basil leaves between the slices. Whisk the olive oil, lemon juice, salt and pepper in a bowl. Drizzle the dressing over the tomatoes and mozzarella. Marinate at room temperature for up to 1 hour for the flavors to blend. Serve at room temperature.

Yield: 4 servings

Papaya with Shrimp and Pomegranate

2 papayas, peeled, halved, seeded
1 pound bay shrimp, cooked, peeled, deveined
1 pomegranate
Bottled raspberry vinaigrette salad dressing
Watercress for garnish

Cut the papayas lengthwise into thin slices and arrange on 8 salad plates. Divide the shrimp evenly between the 8 plates. Split the pomegranate and remove the seeds. Sprinkle 2 tablespoons of seeds on each plate. Warm the raspberry vinaigrette in a small saucepan. Spoon a small amount of vinaigrette over the papaya and shrimp. Garnish with watercress.

Yield: 8 servings

Quick and Easy Focaccia

1 (10-ounce) package refrigerated pizza crust
2 garlic cloves, minced
2/3 cup (2 ounces) grated Romano cheese
2 cups (8 ounces) shredded mozzarella cheese
2 teaspoons oregano
2 firm plum tomatoes, sliced

Roll the pizza dough on a work surface to make a 12-inch circle. Transfer the dough to a pizza pan. Spread the garlic evenly over the dough. Sprinkle with 1/3 cup of the Romano cheese, 1 cup of the mozzarella cheese and 1 teaspoon of the oregano.

Arrange the sliced tomatoes on top. Sprinkle with the remaining 1/3 cup Romano cheese, 1 cup mozzarella cheese and 1 teaspoon oregano. Bake at 375 degrees for 30 to 35 minutes or until golden brown and bubbly. Cut and serve warm.

Yield: 6 servings

Tamale Casserole

1 (15-ounce) can tamales, husks removed
1 (15-ounce) can chili, with or without beans
1/2 can water
1 onion, chopped
3/4 cup crushed corn chips
1 cup shredded Cheddar cheese

Arrange the tamales in the bottom of an 8-inch square baking dish. Spread with the chili and pour the water evenly over the top. Sprinkle with the onion, corn chips and Cheddar cheese in the order listed. Bake at 350 degrees for 30 minutes or until heated through.

Yield: 4 servings

Baked Ziti

Bloom Calendar

A calendar of blooms found in the Willamette Valley includes, but are certainly not limited to:

January: bergenia, helleborus, cyclamen

February: bergenia, helleborus, primrose, camellia

March: bergenia, bluebells, camellia, daffodil, crocus, hyacinth

April: bluebells, tulips, azalea, rhododendron, lilac, hyacinth

May: aster, columbine, dianthus, bleeding heart, lavender, peony, iris, daphne, lily of the valley

June: aster, columbine, clematis, dianthus, bleeding heart, foxglove, geranium, daylily, lobelia, mallow, phlox, rose, fuchsia, hydrangea

(continued on page 65)

1 pound Italian sausage or lean ground beef,
   cooked, drained
1 (48-ounce) jar prepared meatless spaghetti sauce,
   or 6 cups homemade meatless spaghetti sauce
2 teaspoons Italian seasoning
12 ounces ziti, cooked, drained
3 cups shredded mozzarella cheese
1 large egg
2 cups ricotta cheese
1 tablespoon parsley flakes
$1/2$ teaspoon salt (optional)
$1/4$ cup grated Parmesan cheese

Mix the cooked sausage, spaghetti sauce and Italian seasoning in a large bowl. Remove $2^1/2$ cups and set aside. Add the cooked pasta to the remaining sauce and stir to mix. Spread half the pasta mixture in a greased 3- to 4-quart rectangular baking dish. Sprinkle with 1 cup of the mozzarella cheese.

Beat the egg in a medium bowl. Stir in the ricotta cheese, parsley, salt and Parmesan cheese. Spread the ricotta mixture over the mozzarella cheese in the baking dish. Top with the remaining pasta mixture and sprinkle with 1 cup of the mozzarella cheese. Top with the remaining sauce, spreading evenly to the edges of the baking dish.

Bake at 350 degrees for 1 hour or until the center is hot and the edges are bubbly. Remove from the oven and sprinkle with the remaining 1 cup mozzarella cheese. Return to the oven and bake for 5 minutes or until the cheese is melted.

Note: You may eliminate the sausage or ground beef for a vegetarian version.

Yield: 6 to 8 servings

Herb-Stuffed Meat Pie

1 egg
1/4 cup milk
2 1/2 cups herb-seasoned stuffing mix
1 1/2 pounds lean ground beef
1 teaspoon salt (optional)
3 to 4 tablespoons butter
1 onion, chopped
1 apple, peeled, cored, chopped
3 ribs celery, chopped
3 carrots, grated
1/2 cup hot water
Additional butter

Beat the egg and milk in a bowl. Stir in 1/2 cup of the stuffing. Let stand 5 minutes. Add the ground beef and salt and stir to mix. Press the mixture evenly over the bottom and 1/2 inch up the side of a 10-inch pie plate.

Melt 3 to 4 tablespoons butter in a medium skillet. Add the onion, apple, celery and carrots and sauté until the onion is softened. Stir in the water and remaining 2 cups of stuffing. Spoon this mixture into the prepared pie plate. Dot with a little extra butter.

Bake at 350 degrees for 40 to 45 minutes or until the beef is cooked through. Drain excess drippings before cutting into wedges.

Yield: 6 servings

Bloom Calendar

July: aster, astilbe, clematis, daisy, delphinium, dianthus, foxglove, geranium, daylily, lobelia, mallow, phlox, rose, fuchsia, hydrangea

August: anemone, aster, astilbe, clematis, delphinium, foxglove, geranium, daylily, sedum, rose, dahlia, gladiola, heather

September: anemone, aster, chrysanthemum, geranium, daylily, sedum, rose, fuchsia, dahlia

October: anemone, aster, chrysanthemum, sedum, rose

November: chrysanthemum, sedum, rose, winter heather

December: bergenia, helleborus, cyclamen

Tex-Mex Pie

1 pound ground beef
1 onion, chopped
2 tablespoons chili powder
$^1/_2$ envelope taco seasoning mix (optional)
Salt and pepper to taste
1 cup water
1 (8-ounce) can tomato sauce
1 (15-ounce) can creamed corn
2 cups self-rising cornmeal
Boiling water

Brown the ground beef and onion in an ovenproof skillet; drain. Stir in the chili powder and taco seasoning mix and season with salt and pepper. Add 1 cup water and the tomato sauce. Simmer, stirring occasionally, for a few minutes. Add the creamed corn and use a knife to swirl it through the meat mixture. Simmer for a few more minutes.

Mix the cornmeal in a bowl with enough boiling water to make a thick, soupy mixture. Pour the batter evenly over the ground beef mixture. Bake at 500 degrees until the corn bread topping is golden brown. Cut into wedges and serve from the skillet.

Yield: 4 to 6 servings

The Oregon coast is legendary for its windswept scenery, charming lighthouses, endless beaches and seaside towns.

Baked Chicken Dijon

1/2 cup (1 stick) butter
2 garlic cloves, minced
5 teaspoons Dijon mustard
1 1/2 cups bread crumbs
5 tablespoons grated Parmesan cheese
2 tablespoons finely chopped fresh parsley
4 boneless chicken breasts, pounded to 1/2-inch thickness

Melt the butter in a saucepan over low heat. Add the garlic and simmer for 5 minutes. Stir in the mustard. Remove from the heat and let cool to lukewarm. Whisk mixture until thickened.

Mix the bread crumbs, Parmesan cheese and parsley in a pie plate. Dip the chicken breasts in the butter mixture and then in the bread crumbs. Pat the bread crumbs onto the chicken to coat well. Place in a 10x15-inch baking pan.

Cover and chill for several hours to set the breading. Remove the chicken breasts to a second 10x15-inch baking pan. Bake at 350 degrees for 15 minutes or until cooked through.

Yield: 4 servings

State Capital: *Salem*
State Flower: *Oregon Grape*
State Tree: *Douglas Fir*
State Bird: *Western Meadowlark*
State Animal: *Beaver*
State Fish: *Chinook Salmon*
State Rock: *Thunдеregg*
State Gem: *Sunstone*
State Insect: *Swallowtail Butterfly*
State Dance: *Square Dance*
State Beverage: *Milk*
State Mushroom: *Pacific Golden Chanterelle*

Roasted Chicken

1 or 2 whole roasting hens
Fresh or dried thyme to taste
Fresh or dried tarragon to taste
Fresh or dried parsley to taste
Salt and pepper to taste

Place the chicken in a roasting pan. Coat with nonstick cooking spray. Sprinkle generously with thyme, tarragon, parsley, salt and pepper. Roast at 350 degrees for 1 1/2 to 3 hours or until cooked through and the skin is golden brown and slightly crispy.

Yield: 1 or 2 roasted chickens

Easy Aromatic Turkey

1/2 cup (1 stick) butter or margarine, melted
1 garlic clove, minced
1/2 teaspoon tarragon
1/2 teaspoon thyme
1/2 teaspoon rosemary
1 (2- to 3-pound) turkey breast
6 red potatoes
6 carrots
Onions (optional)
Celery (optional)
1/2 cup chicken broth

Mix the melted butter, garlic, tarragon, thyme and rosemary in a small bowl. Place the turkey breast in a roasting pan. Drizzle half the butter mixture over the turkey.

Roast, uncovered, at 375 degrees for 30 minutes. Add the potatoes, carrots, onions, celery and chicken broth. Drizzle the remaining butter mixture over the turkey and vegetables. Cover and roast for 45 minutes or until the turkey is cooked through.

Yield: 4 to 6 servings

Sautéed Scallops with Lime

3 tablespoons olive oil
1 1/2 pounds sea scallops
2 tablespoons finely chopped fresh cilantro
1 garlic clove, minced
1 teaspoon fresh lime juice
Salt and freshly ground pepper to taste

Heat the olive oil in a large nonstick skillet over medium-high heat until almost smoking. Add the scallops and cook for 2 minutes or until browned on the bottom. Turn the scallops over and cook for 2 minutes or until opaque through the center. Add the cilantro, garlic and lime juice. Season with salt and pepper. Toss to mix and remove from the heat. Serve with crusty bread and a salad.

Yield: 2 to 4 servings

Broccoli Bake

1 (10 3/4-ounce) can cream of mushroom soup
2 eggs, slightly beaten
1 cup shredded Cheddar cheese
1 cup mayonnaise
2 tablespoons finely chopped onion
1 cup butter cracker crumbs
2 cups chopped fresh broccoli or 2 (10-ounce) packages
    frozen chopped broccoli, thawed, drained

Mix the soup, eggs, Cheddar cheese, mayonnaise and onion in a large bowl. Add the cracker crumbs and broccoli and stir to mix well. Spoon into a 9x13-inch baking dish. Bake at 325 degrees for 45 minutes.

Note: You may substitute zucchini, green beans, cauliflower or other vegetables in place of the broccoli.

Yield: 8 servings

Glazed Carrots with Pecans

1/4 cup pecan halves
11/2 cups baby carrots
2 tablespoons butter
1/4 cup packed brown sugar
1/8 teaspoon ground cloves

Spread the pecans in a shallow baking pan. Bake at 350 degrees until lightly toasted, shaking the pan often to prevent burning. Remove to a cutting board and coarsely chop the pecans. Cook the carrots in a steamer for 10 minutes or until tender-crisp. Melt the butter in a saucepan. Stir in the carrots, brown sugar and cloves. Cook until heated through. Stir in the pecans and serve.

Yield: 4 servings

Colonial Green Beans and Bacon

4 slices bacon
1 (9-ounce) package frozen Italian-style green beans, thawed, drained
3 carrots, thinly sliced
1 tablespoon butter or margarine
1 garlic clove, minced
1/4 teaspoon pepper

Fry the bacon in a skillet until crisp. Remove with a slotted spoon to paper towels to drain. Remove all but 1 tablespoon of the bacon drippings from the skillet. Add the beans, carrots, butter and garlic. Stir-fry over medium-high heat for 5 minutes or until the vegetables are tender-crisp. Crumble the bacon and add it to the skillet. Stir in the pepper and serve.

Note: You may substitute fresh green beans, with stems removed, in place of the frozen green beans.

Yield: 4 servings

Fresh Green Beans with Country Almond Butter

2 pounds Blue Lake green beans, trimmed
1/3 cup butter
1 cup slivered almonds, toasted
1 tablespoon whole-grain mustard
1 tablespoon honey
1 tablespoon grated lemon zest
1 tablespoon fresh lemon juice
2 tablespoons minced shallots or red onion
1 teaspoon minced garlic
Salt and pepper to taste

Blanch the beans in lightly salted boiling water in a saucepan for 3 to 4 minutes or until tender-crisp and bright green. Plunge the beans into ice water. Drain when cool.

Melt the butter in a large heavy skillet over medium heat. Add the almonds, mustard, honey, lemon zest, lemon juice, shallots and garlic and sauté for 2 to 3 minutes. Stir in the beans and cook for 3 to 5 minutes or until heated through. Season with salt and pepper and serve immediately.

Yield: 6 to 8 servings

Haystack Rock at Cannon Beach is the world's third largest freestanding monolith.

Scalloped Potato Casserole

1 cup sour cream
1 (10³/4-ounce) can cream of mushroom soup
1/4 cup (1/2 stick) butter or margarine, melted
1/4 cup sliced green onions
1¹/2 cups shredded Cheddar cheese
3 pounds potatoes, peeled, boiled, cubed
1 teaspoon pepper
1/2 teaspoon salt
1/2 cup bread crumbs

Mix the sour cream, soup, butter, green onions and 1 cup of the Cheddar cheese in a large bowl. Stir in the potatoes, pepper and salt. Spoon into a 3-quart baking dish. Top with the bread crumbs and remaining 1/2 cup Cheddar cheese. Bake at 350 degrees for 30 to 35 minutes.

Yield: 8 servings

Herbed Rice

1/4 cup (1/2 stick) butter or margarine
1 cup uncooked rice
2¹/2 cups chicken broth
3 tablespoons instant minced onion
1 teaspoon salt
1/2 teaspoon rosemary
1/2 teaspoon marjoram
1/2 teaspoon thyme

Combine the butter, rice, broth, onion, salt, rosemary, marjoram and thyme in a saucepan. Bring to a boil over medium heat. Stir once and reduce the heat. Cover and simmer for 14 to 20 minutes or until the rice is tender and the liquid is absorbed.

Yield: 4 to 6 servings

Zucchini Stir-Fry with Garlic and Lime

1 pound zucchini (about 4 small)
3/4 teaspoon salt
1 tablespoon butter or margarine
1 tablespoon olive oil
4 to 5 garlic cloves, thinly sliced
1 tablespoon fresh lime juice
1/4 teaspoon freshly ground pepper
1/2 teaspoon oregano
2 tablespoons chopped fresh Italian flat-leaf parsley
Salt to taste

Trim the ends from the zucchini and cut into 1/2-inch cubes. Toss the zucchini with 3/4 teaspoon salt in a bowl. Remove to a colander and let drain for 30 minutes in the sink. Rinse and pat dry.

Heat the butter and olive oil in a large skillet or wok over medium-low heat. Add the garlic and sauté until the garlic is golden brown. Do not let the garlic burn. Remove with a slotted spoon to paper towels to drain.

Increase the heat to medium-high. Add the zucchini and stir-fry for 5 to 8 minutes or until golden brown and tender-crisp. Stir in the garlic, lime juice, pepper, oregano and parsley. Season with salt and serve.

Yield: 4 servings

Oregon Berry Cobbler

Blackberries

Near Eugene, in a state park honoring Elijah Bristow, Lane County's first settler, an easy trail offers an especially fun hike with children in August, when masses of sweet juicy blackberries ripen along the trail. Equestrians share the trail, delighting children who fill their buckets and tummies with the juicy berries and watch the horses stroll along the same trail.

When the August heat breaks a sweat on the blackberry pickers, an inviting swimming hole nearby offers a cooling respite where the kids can frolic. Back home, the blackberries can be made into jams and cobblers or spooned over ice cream for a perfect summertime treat.

5 cups fresh or frozen blackberries or marionberries
  (about 1³/4 pounds)
³/4 cup sugar
2 tablespoons flour
1 teaspoon grated lemon zest
1 tablespoon fresh lemon juice
1 teaspoon vanilla extract
1 cup flour
¹/2 teaspoon baking powder
¹/2 teaspoon baking soda
¹/2 cup plain nonfat yogurt
2 tablespoons fresh lemon juice
2 tablespoons butter or margarine, melted
1 teaspoon vanilla extract
2 egg whites

Combine the berries, sugar, 2 tablespoons flour, lemon zest, 1 tablespoon lemon juice and 1 teaspoon vanilla in a bowl. Toss gently to coat the berries. Spoon into a 7x11-inch baking dish coated with nonstick cooking spray.

Mix 1 cup flour, baking powder and baking soda in a bowl. Mix the yogurt, 2 tablespoons lemon juice, melted butter, 1 teaspoon vanilla and egg whites in a separate bowl. Add the yogurt mixture to the dry ingredients and stir until just moistened. Drop the dough by tablespoons on top of the berry mixture.

Bake at 400 degrees for 30 minutes or until the filling is bubbly and the crust is golden brown.

Yield: 8 servings

Gingersnap Pears

4 firm ripe pears
$^1/_4$ cup orange juice
$^1/_2$ cup finely crushed gingersnaps (about 8 cookies)
2 tablespoons sugar
2 tablespoons chopped walnuts
2 tablespoons butter or margarine, melted
Half-and-half or vanilla ice cream

Peel, halve and core the pears. Arrange the pear halves cut side up, in a $7^1/_2$x12-inch baking dish coated with nonstick cooking spray. Drizzle with the orange juice. Mix the gingersnaps, sugar, walnuts and melted butter in a small bowl. Sprinkle evenly over the pears. Bake at 350 degrees for 20 to 25 minutes or until the pears are tender. Serve warm topped with half-and-half or ice cream.

Yield: 8 servings

Peanut Butter Pie

$^3/_4$ cup confectioners' sugar
8 ounces cream cheese, softened
8 ounces nondairy whipped topping
$^1/_2$ cup milk
1 cup creamy or chunky peanut butter
1 baked (9-inch) pie shell or 1 (9-inch) graham cracker pie shell

Combine the confectioners' sugar, cream cheese, whipped topping, milk and peanut butter in a bowl. Stir until well mixed. Pour into the pie shell. Chill for several hours or until firm.

Yield: 8 servings

Fresh Fruit Tart

$^3/_4$ cup (1$^1/_2$ sticks) butter, softened
1$^1/_2$ cups sugar
1 teaspoon vanilla extract
3 cups flour
1 teaspoon baking powder
$^1/_2$ teaspoon salt
16 ounces cream cheese, softened
$^1/_2$ (14-ounce) can sweetened condensed milk
Fresh grapes, blueberries, sliced kiwi, sliced strawberries or other fruit
2 tablespoons orange marmalade

Beat the butter, sugar and vanilla in a mixing bowl until smooth. Mix the flour, baking powder and salt in a bowl. Add the dry ingredients to the butter mixture and stir to form a dough. Pat the dough into the bottom of a pizza pan. Bake at 375 degrees for 10 minutes or until lightly browned. Remove to a wire rack to cool completely.

Mix the cream cheese and sweetened condensed milk in a bowl. Spread evenly over the baked crust. Arrange the fruit on top. Mix the marmalade with a small amount of water in a bowl to thin slightly. Drizzle over the fruit. Chill the tart completely. Cut into wedges and serve.

Yield: 12 to 16 servings

Mixed Nut Squares

3/4 cup packed brown sugar
1/3 cup butter, softened
1 teaspoon vanilla extract
1 egg yolk
2 cups baking mix
1/2 cup light corn syrup
2 tablespoons butter
1 cup (6 ounces) butterscotch chips
1 (12-ounce) can mixed nuts

Combine the brown sugar, 1/3 cup butter, vanilla, egg yolk and baking mix in a bowl. Mix with a fork to form a dough. Press into a 9x13-inch ungreased baking dish. Bake at 350 degrees for 15 to 20 minutes. Remove to a wire rack to cool.

Combine the corn syrup, 2 tablespoons butter and butterscotch chips in a saucepan. Cook over medium heat until melted, stirring frequently. Pour over the cooled crust. Sprinkle the nuts evenly over the top and press into the butterscotch mixture. Cut into 1-inch squares when cool.

Yield: 9 to 10 dozen squares

The Three Sisters Mountains, all over 10,000 feet, bear more than a dozen glaciers.

Coastal Getaways

The Oregon Coast abounds with fresh seafood year-round! The northern coastal towns of Astoria and Pacific City provide residents with fresh crab, oysters, and a wide variety of local fish. As the mighty Columbia River spills out into the sea, salmon and halibut cross the bar in an endless cycle of renewal. In the central coastal cities of Lincoln City, Newport, and Florence, any time of year is a good time to visit the docks. Fresh seasonal tuna, halibut, and shark are a must-have. The towns of Gold Beach and Brookings on the very southern coast of Oregon enjoy beautiful weather most of the year, making crabbing and fishing a perfect way to spend the day.

Each recipe in Coastal Getaways was selected for its great taste and unique representation of all that is Oregon seafood: fresh, plentiful, and right for any occasion. Whether your menu includes Ginger Salmon for a summer lunch with friends, or Margarita Shrimp to begin a romantic evening on a cold and stormy night, you will find just the right selection in this chapter.

Oregon is a delight for seafood lovers. The tempting recipes in this chapter speak to Oregon's rich coastal lifestyle and love of food. It is our pleasure to share them with you.

Oceanside beach, Tillamook County, Oregon

photo by Bruce Berg

Coastal Getaways *Contents*

Shrimp with Garlic

1 teaspoon salt
1 cup water
12 ounces medium uncooked shrimp, peeled, deveined
$1/2$ cup extra-virgin olive oil
1 tablespoon minced garlic
$1/2$ teaspoon crushed red pepper
1 teaspoon balsamic vinegar
$1/4$ cup chopped fresh parsley

Dissolve the salt in the water in a medium bowl. Add the shrimp and let soak for 5 minutes. Drain and pat dry with paper towels.

Heat the olive oil in a medium skillet over medium-high heat until hot but not smoking. Add the shrimp in a single layer and sprinkle with the garlic and red pepper. Cook for 1 minute. Turn the shrimp over with tongs. Cook for 1 minute or until just pink and opaque throughout. Do not overcook. Remove from the heat. Stir in the vinegar and parsley and serve.

Yield: 8 to 10 servings

More than a thousand varieties of old garden roses
bloom in Newberg's Heirloom Old Rose Garden.

Margarita Shrimp

1^1/$_2$ pounds (26 to 30) large uncooked shrimp, peeled, deveined
^{1}/$_4$ cup fresh lime juice
^{1}/$_4$ cup tequila
^{1}/$_4$ cup water
^{1}/$_4$ cup finely chopped onion
1 tablespoon olive oil
^{1}/$_4$ teaspoon salt
Hot cooked brown or white rice, enough for 4 servings
Lime slices for garnish

Place the shrimp in a shallow glass dish. Mix the lime juice, tequila, water, onion, olive oil and salt in a bowl. Pour over the shrimp. Marinate for 10 to 15 minutes.

Remove the shrimp and thread onto 4 skewers, running the skewer twice through each shrimp. Pour the marinade into a saucepan. Bring to a boil and simmer for 5 minutes. Remove from the heat and keep warm.

Coat a hot grill with nonstick cooking spray. Place the shrimp on the grill and cook for 3 minutes per side or until opaque throughout. Remove the shrimp from the skewers and arrange on the cooked rice on serving plates. Drizzle with the warm marinade and garnish with lime slices.

Yield: 4 servings

Seaside Clam Chowder

4 slices bacon
1/2 cup finely chopped onion
4 medium potatoes, peeled, diced
1 tablespoon flour
2 (6-ounce) cans minced clams with liquid, or
    2 to 3 dozen fresh clams
1 (8-ounce) bottle clam juice
1 cup half-and-half
Salt and pepper to taste
1/2 cup heavy cream (optional)
2 tablespoons chopped fresh parsley

Cook the bacon in a large heavy saucepan until crisp. Remove and drain on paper towels. Chop or crumble the bacon. Add the onion and potatoes to the bacon drippings in the saucepan. Sauté for a few minutes.

Sprinkle the flour into the saucepan and stir in the liquid from the canned clams and the bottled clam juice. Bring to a boil. Reduce the heat and simmer, stirring occasionally, for 15 minutes or until the potatoes are tender.

If using fresh clams, wash the clams and place in a steamer. Steam until the shells open. Discard any unopened clams. Remove the clams from the shells and mince. Add the canned or fresh minced clams to the saucepan. Stir in the half-and-half and season with salt and pepper. Heat to simmering but do not boil. Stir in the heavy cream. Sprinkle with the fresh parsley and crumbled bacon and serve.

Yield: 6 servings

Cape Perpetua

We strapped the baby in the backpack and headed down the lush fern-lined trail with our four-year-old. A sweeping coastline vista greeted us as we emerged from the forest. The sun cast light brilliantly off the whitecaps on the ocean. Tidepools galore beckoned us to come explore. We petted starfish, gently poked a few sea anemones, and also admired, but did not touch, a sea urchin just under the waves.

Hermit crabs crawled from tidepool to tidepool on some unexplained journey, carrying their seashell homes behind them. We turned and gazed up at the tall trees lining the hillside, standing almost as if they are guarding this spot. Cape Perpetua will always entertain a family for an afternoon.

Simple Seafood Soup

"Green Flash" on Ocean

Waves lap the tide pools as a light breeze flutters beach grasses along the shoreline. A pelican swoops into the water picking up a fish dinner in his bill. Smells of barbecue fill the air: sweet, smoky, tantalizing. Sipping wine, we sit on worn wooden chairs, watch the sun make its descent into the Pacific, and ponder the legend of the "green flash."

Apparently, when the sun sets on the horizon, just after ducking under the ocean from view, you see a flash of brilliant green light. We gaze westward, the sun creeping down into the Pacific, until only its tip is visible. Suddenly, for an instant, bright florescent green light appears, unlike any color ever painted. Another perfect day ends along the Oregon Coast.

2 tablespoons vegetable or olive oil
1 large onion, chopped
2 garlic cloves, minced
1 teaspoon basil
$1/2$ teaspoon oregano
$1/4$ teaspoon pepper
Chopped fresh parsley to taste
1 (46-ounce) can tomato juice
1 (15-ounce) can Italian-style tomatoes
1 (7-ounce) can tuna
1 (15-ounce) can green beans, drained
1 (7-ounce) can minced clams
1 (6-ounce) can shrimp or 1 cup cooked, peeled, deveined shrimp
Grated Parmesan cheese (optional)

Heat the oil in a large saucepan. Add the onion and sauté until softened. Add the garlic and sauté for 1 to 2 minutes. Stir in the basil, oregano and pepper. Sprinkle with the fresh parsley.

Stir in the tomato juice, tomatoes, tuna, green beans, clams and shrimp. Let simmer for at least 30 minutes. Ladle into bowls and sprinkle with Parmesan cheese.

Yield: 6 servings

Bread Salad

4 ripe Roma tomatoes, diced
1 teaspoon salt
2 green onions, sliced lengthwise, coarsely chopped
2 tablespoons olive oil
1 Anaheim chile, seeded, diced
10 fresh basil leaves
1 loaf two-day-old Panzanella or other hearty Italian bread, sliced
1 tablespoon water
Julienned fresh basil leaves for garnish

Mix the tomatoes and salt in a large bowl. Add the green onions, olive oil, chile and basil leaves and toss to mix. Let stand for 1 hour. Alternate layers of bread slices with the tomato mixture on a serving platter. Sprinkle with the water. Garnish with fresh basil and serve.

Yield: 4 servings

Cranberry Salad

^{1}/4 cup frozen cranberry juice cocktail concentrate, thawed
^{1}/4 cup rice wine vinegar
1^1/2 teaspoons Dijon mustard
^{1}/4 teaspoon pepper
^{1}/2 cup vegetable oil
1 bunch fresh spinach, rinsed well, dried
2 pears, cored, sliced
^{1}/2 red onion, sliced
1 cup dried cranberries
^{1}/2 cup feta cheese
1 avocado, peeled, pitted, sliced

Whisk the cranberry juice cocktail, vinegar, mustard, pepper and oil in a small bowl. Cover and chill the dressing. Combine the spinach, pears, onion, cranberries, feta cheese and avocado in a large bowl. Add the dressing and toss to mix.

Yield: 4 to 6 servings

Farm Fresh Tomato and Cucumber Salad

Dressing
1/4 cup balsamic vinegar
1/2 cup olive oil
1 garlic clove, minced
Salt and freshly ground pepper to taste

Salad
2 to 3 ripe tomatoes, cut into quarters or eighths
2 to 3 cucumbers, peeled, sliced
7 to 8 fresh basil leaves

For the dressing, whisk the vinegar, olive oil and garlic in a small bowl. Season with salt and pepper.

For the salad, combine the tomatoes and cucumbers in a medium bowl. Add the dressing. Cut the basil leaves into strips with kitchen shears and add to the salad. Toss to mix. Cover and chill.

Yield: 4 servings

Oregon currently has more than 900 Century Farms and Ranches—family operated continuously for 100 years or more.

Crunchy Shrimp Salad

Dressing

$1/2$ cup mayonnaise or mayonnaise-type salad dressing
1 tablespoon lemon juice
1 tablespoon soy sauce
$1/4$ teaspoon grated fresh gingerroot or
    dried ground ginger

Salad

8 ounces small to medium cooked shrimp, peeled,
    deveined, chilled
1 cup fresh bean sprouts
1 (4-ounce) can sliced water chestnuts, drained
$1/4$ cup chopped green onions
$1/4$ cup chopped celery
1 (5-ounce) can chow mein noodles

For the dressing, mix the mayonnaise, lemon juice, soy sauce and gingerroot in a small bowl. Cover and chill.

For the salad, mix the shrimp, bean sprouts, water chestnuts, green onions and celery in a medium bowl. Cover and chill. Add the dressing and chow mein noodles to the shrimp mixture. Toss to mix and serve.

Yield: 4 servings

Face Rock

Looking longingly to the heavens, he does not change his glance. Alone he sits, day after day, the ocean intermittently hugging and releasing him. Seagulls visit but never stay long. Sand envelops him constantly like a tattered security blanket.

He does not move, even as the wind blows over him and rain pelts him from above. He does not care that mere mortals stare at him in amazement and question his existence. He knows he has always been in this place and he will be here even after those people have vanished. He is only a profile, but we are awe-struck and bewildered by him nonetheless. He resides in the Pacific Ocean at Bandon-by-the-Sea. He is the man we call Face Rock.

Hood River Applesauce Bread

Shore Acres State Park

Cheerful carols greet your ears as cascading holiday lights weave a glow through pathways of flower gardens. The aroma of cinnamon and apples wafts from the decorative, historic Simpson House. A myriad of photos and articles detail the Simpson family's founding of these gardens overlooking the Pacific Ocean. Perusing as you sip hot apple cider, the transformation of these beautiful grounds over time is amazing.

Outside, you sit on a bench watching dancing lights over a garden pond. Isn't it marvelous how many wedding vows are exchanged in this exact locale? How magnificent these gardens must be in spring and summer, their colored lights of flowers blooming. Glancing around while finishing your cider, you anticipate a return to see other seasonal delights at Shore Acres State Park.

4 cups flour
2 tablespoons cornstarch
2 cups sugar
4 teaspoons baking soda
1 teaspoon cinnamon
$1/2$ teaspoon ground cloves
$1/2$ teaspoon allspice
$1/2$ teaspoon nutmeg
$1/4$ teaspoon salt
1 cup vegetable oil
3 cups applesauce
1 cup raisins
$1/2$ cup chopped walnuts

Mix the flour, cornstarch, sugar, baking soda, cinnamon, cloves, allspice, nutmeg and salt in a large bowl.

Mix the oil, applesauce, raisins and walnuts in a medium bowl. Add to the dry ingredients and stir to mix well. Divide the batter between 2 greased 5x9-inch loaf pans.

Bake at 350 degrees for 1 hour or until a wooden pick inserted in the center comes out clean. Cool in the pans for 10 minutes. Invert the bread onto wire racks and let cool completely.

Yield: 2 loaves

Orange Rolls

Rolls
1¹/₄ cups scalded milk
¹/₂ cup (1 stick) butter, softened
¹/₃ cup sugar
1 teaspoon salt
1 cake yeast
2 eggs, well beaten
2 tablespoons grated orange zest
¹/₄ cup orange juice
5 cups flour

Orange Glaze
1 teaspoon grated orange zest
2 tablespoons orange juice
1 cup confectioners' sugar

For the bread, mix the milk, butter, sugar and salt in a large bowl. Stir until the sugar dissolves. Let cool to lukewarm. Add the yeast and let soften. Beat in the eggs, orange zest and orange juice. Beat in the flour gradually. Cover and let stand for 10 minutes. Turn out on a floured surface and knead lightly. Place in a greased bowl and turn to coat. Cover with a damp cloth. Let rise in a warm place for 2 hours or until doubled in bulk. Punch down and let rest for 2 minutes.

Place the dough on a lightly floured surface. Roll out the dough. Cut into ¹/₂x4-inch strips. Tie each strip in a knot and place 2 inches apart on a greased baking sheet. Cover with a damp cloth and let rise in a warm place for 1 hour or until doubled in bulk. Bake at 375 degrees for 15 to 20 minutes or until golden brown. Remove to a wire rack and let cool slightly.

For the glaze, mix the orange zest, orange juice and confectioners' sugar in a small bowl. Drizzle over the warm rolls and serve with butter.

Yield: 3 dozen rolls

Pacific Coast Halibut with Yogurt Topping

2 pounds halibut fillets
Salt and pepper to taste
^{1}/2 cup plain nonfat yogurt
1 teaspoon fresh lemon juice
1 tablespoon light mayonnaise
^{1}/4 teaspoon dillweed
^{1}/2 cup peeled, chopped cucumber
^{1}/4 cup pitted sliced green olives
2 tablespoons chopped fresh parsley

Place the halibut fillets in a 9x9-inch baking dish coated with nonstick cooking spray. Season with salt and pepper. Mix the yogurt, lemon juice, mayonnaise, dillweed, cucumber, olives and parsley in a bowl. Spread evenly over the fillets. Bake at 425 degrees for 15 minutes or until the fish flakes easily.

Yield: 4 servings

Red Snapper with Herb Crust

^{1}/2 loaf French bread, cubed
2 slices bacon, cooked crisp, drained
2 teaspoons chopped fresh basil leaves
2 teaspoons chopped fresh chives
2 teaspoons chopped fresh parsley
6 red snapper fillets
^{1}/2 cup olive oil

Process the bread, bacon, basil, chives and parsley in a food processor until crumbly. Remove to a plate. Pour the olive oil into a shallow bowl. Coat the fillets in the olive oil and then in the bread crumb mixture. Pat the bread crumbs onto the fillets to coat well. Arrange the fillets in a greased 9x13-inch baking dish. Bake at 400 degrees for 15 minutes or until the fish flakes easily.

Yield: 6 servings

Ginger Salmon with Kiwi Salsa

Ginger Salmon
4 salmon fillets
2 tablespoons thinly sliced fresh gingerroot
2 tablespoons chopped green onions
Soy sauce
4 teaspoons vegetable oil (optional)

Kiwi Salsa
6 ripe kiwifruit, peeled, diced
2 tablespoons minced red onion
1/2 teaspoon finely chopped jalapeño chile
2 tablespoons finely chopped fresh cilantro
2 teaspoons grated lime zest
2 tablespoons (or more) fresh lime juice
1/2 teaspoon (or more) salt

For the salmon, rinse the salmon fillets and pat dry. Arrange on a microwave-safe plate. Sprinkle with the sliced gingerroot and green onions. Top each with a splash of soy sauce. Cover the plate with plastic wrap, venting one edge. Microwave on High for 7 minutes or until the fish flakes easily. Heat the oil in a small microwave-safe dish on High for 30 seconds or until hot. Drizzle the hot oil over the salmon.

For the salsa, mix the kiwifruit, red onion, jalapeño, cilantro, lime zest, lime juice and salt in a bowl. Add more lime juice or salt if desired. Serve with Ginger Salmon.

Note: You may substitute pineapple in place of the kiwifruit if kiwifruit is not in season. May also serve the salsa with chicken or tortilla chips.

Yield: 4 servings

Be Careful What You Wish For

"Wouldn't it be neat if the lights went out?" exclaimed one of the children at the dinner table.

"Nooooo!" responded the adults in unison.

No sooner had the exchange taken place than everything went dead. No lights. No TV. No heaters. No fan to spread the fireplace's heat. Nothing but the weak signal from a battery-operated radio reporting a dark and stormy night at the coast!

Not long after we finished our meal by candlelight, the children's excitement for "roughing it" was replaced by bone-chilling cold. We gathered every blanket we could find, piled into beds, and invited sleep to dull the raging wind and rain outside.

At 2:00 a.m., when exhaustion had just brought slumber, power was restored and every light and electrical device we'd forgotten to turn "off" simultaneously went "on." Needless to say, when morning arrived, we slept in, ate a wonderful breakfast, and didn't wish for a thing.

Champagne Risotto with Scallops

2 tablespoons olive oil
1/4 cup chopped shallots
1/2 teaspoon thyme
2 cups fresh arugula leaves
2 cups arborio rice
1/2 cup Champagne
7 cups (about) hot chicken stock
Salt and pepper to taste
1 pound small scallops or large quartered scallops
1/2 cup chopped chives
2 tablespoons balsamic vinegar

Heat the olive oil in a large saucepan. Stir in the shallots and thyme and cook for 2 minutes. Add the arugula and cook until just wilted. Add the rice and cook, stirring frequently, until the rice is translucent. Add the Champagne and cook, stirring constantly, until almost evaporated.

Add 1 cup of the stock to the saucepan. Cook, stirring, until the liquid is absorbed. Add the remaining stock 1 cup at a time, cooking and stirring until the liquid is absorbed before adding more. Taste the rice after the sixth cup of stock has been added, as the rice should be almost done. Season with salt and pepper.

Stir the scallops into the rice mixture. Cook for 1 minute and remove from the heat. Let stand for 3 minutes, as the scallops will continue to cook. Stir in the chives and vinegar and serve.

Note: You may substitute fresh baby spinach leaves or watercress in place of the arugula.

Yield: 4 servings

Roasted Cranberry Relish

1 pound fresh cranberries
2 tablespoons water
1^1/$_2$ cups sugar
^{1}/$_4$ cup lemon juice
1 (8-ounce) jar orange marmalade
^{1}/$_4$ teaspoon ginger
Grated lemon zest for garnish

Wash and dry the cranberries. Spread evenly in a 9x13-inch baking pan. Sprinkle with the water and then the sugar. Cover with foil and bake at 325 degrees for 30 to 40 minutes or until the cranberries pop. Shake the pan once or twice during baking. Stir in the lemon juice, marmalade and ginger. Spoon into a medium bowl and let cool. Cover and chill. Garnish with grated lemon zest and serve.

Yield: 12 to 14 servings

Crispy Twice-Baked Potatoes

^{1}/$_2$ cup olive oil
6 garlic cloves, minced
20 new potatoes, cut into eighths
2 teaspoons Salad Supreme seasoning blend

Pour the olive oil into a 4-quart microwave-safe covered baking dish. Stir in the garlic. Add the potatoes and stir to coat. Cover and microwave on High for 5 minutes, stirring halfway through. Remove to a baking sheet and arrange in a single layer. Sprinkle with the Salad Supreme seasoning. Bake at 350 degrees for 40 minutes or until golden brown, stirring every 10 minutes.

Yield: 6 servings

Chanterelle-Stuffed Tomatoes

4 ripe tomatoes
1 tablespoon butter
Salt and pepper to taste
4 slices bacon, diced
1 pound fresh chanterelle mushrooms
$^1\!/_2$ cup finely chopped onion
Pinch of chili powder
$^1\!/_4$ cup (or more) sour cream
Buttered bread crumbs

Cut a slice from the stem end of the tomatoes. Remove the seeds and pulp and reserve the pulp. Divide the butter between the 4 tomato cavities. Season with salt and pepper.

Fry the bacon in a skillet until crisp. Remove with a slotted spoon to paper towels to drain. Add the mushrooms and onion to the bacon drippings in the skillet. Sauté for 5 minutes. Stir in the reserved tomato pulp. Cook until the mixture is almost dry. Add the cooked bacon and a pinch of chili powder. Season with salt and pepper. Stir in the sour cream to bind the mixture. Fill the tomato cavities with the mushroom mixture. Top with buttered bread crumbs. Bake at 350 degrees for 20 to 30 minutes.

Yield: 4 servings

Orange Pilaf

$^3\!/_4$ cup (1$^1\!/_2$ sticks) butter
$^1\!/_2$ cup chopped celery
$^1\!/_4$ cup sliced green onion tops
1 cup uncooked long grain white rice
1 cup orange juice
1 cup water
1 orange, peeled, seeded, chopped
$^1\!/_4$ cup slivered almonds

Melt the butter in a saucepan. Add the celery and green onions and sauté until the vegetables are softened. Add the rice and sauté for 4 to 5 minutes. Stir in the orange juice and water. Cover and simmer for 25 minutes or until the rice is tender and the liquid is absorbed. Fold in the chopped orange and almonds and serve hot.

Yield: 4 servings

Angel Hair Pasta with Crab and Filberts

1/4 cup (1/2 stick) unsalted butter
1/2 cup chopped toasted peeled filberts
Grated zest of 2 large or 3 small lemons
3/4 cup chardonnay
2 tablespoons unsalted butter
3/4 pound crab meat, drained, flaked
Salt and freshly ground black pepper to taste
12 ounces fresh angel hair pasta
Fresh chopped chives
Lemon wedges for garnish

Melt 1/4 cup butter in a large skillet. Add the filberts and cook over low heat for 1 minute. Stir in the lemon zest and cook for 1 minute. Stir in the chardonnay and bring to a boil. Boil for 5 minutes or until the liquid is reduced by half.

Add 2 tablespoons butter to the skillet and cook until melted. Reduce the heat and stir in the crab meat. Season with salt and pepper. Cook until heated through.

Cook the pasta in a large saucepan of boiling salted water for 1 minute or until just tender. Drain well. Toss the pasta and crab sauce in a large serving bowl. Season with pepper and sprinkle with chives. Serve garnished with lemon wedges.

Yield: 4 servings

Crabbing

Crabbing along the Oregon Coast is an entertaining way to take in the natural beauty of Oregon's unique coastline. The only thing better than tossing out the traps with the seagulls swooping and diving, the salt smell of the Pacific Ocean, and a light wind blowing, is the excitement of pulling up the traps to discover a bounty of large Dungeness crabs.

After a successful haul, the tastebuds anticipate the cooked crab that has been cracked and spread out on a newspaper and accompanied with melted butter or a spicy cocktail sauce, crusty French bread, and cold pale amber microbrew. Between mouthfuls, family and friends reminisce about a wonderful day spent on the Oregon Coast.

Fresh Fruit Pie

1/4 cup cornstarch
3/4 cup cold water
1 1/3 cups sugar
1/2 cup water
1/8 teaspoon salt

1 tablespoon lemon juice
6 cups fresh blueberries or sliced
   fresh peaches
2 baked (9-inch) pie shells

Dissolve the cornstarch in 3/4 cup cold water in a small bowl. Combine the sugar and 1/2 cup water in a saucepan. Bring to a boil. Add the dissolved cornstarch. Cook, stirring often, until clear and thick. Stir in the salt and lemon juice. Remove from the heat and let cool for a few minutes. Fold in the fresh fruit. Divide the fruit mixture between the 2 baked pie shells. Chill for at least 3 hours before serving.

Yield: 12 servings

Lemon Melt-Aways

Cookies
1 1/4 cups flour
3/4 cup (1 1/2 sticks) butter,
   softened
1/2 cup cornstarch
1/3 cup confectioners' sugar
1 teaspoon grated lemon zest
1 tablespoon fresh lemon juice

Lemon Frosting
3/4 cup confectioners' sugar
1/4 cup (1/2 stick) butter, softened
1 teaspoon grated lemon zest
1 tablespoon fresh lemon juice

For the cookies, combine the flour, butter, cornstarch, confectioners' sugar, lemon zest and lemon juice in a mixing bowl. Beat at low speed for 2 to 3 minutes or until well mixed. Scrape down the sides of the bowl often while beating. Turn the dough onto a work surface. Divide in half and shape each half into an 1x8-inch roll. Wrap each roll in plastic wrap and chill for 1 to 2 hours or until firm.

Cut each roll into 1/4-inch slices. Place the slices 2 inches apart on cookie sheets. Bake at 350 degrees for 8 to 12 minutes or until set. The cookies will not be brown. Remove to a wire rack and let cool.

For the frosting, combine the confectioners' sugar, butter, lemon zest and lemon juice in a small mixing bowl. Beat at medium speed for 1 to 2 minutes or until fluffy. Scrape down the sides of the bowl often while beating. Frost the cooled cookies.

Yield: 5 dozen cookies

Sleeping Lady Brownies

Brownies
2 cups (4 sticks) butter
1¹/2 pounds semisweet chocolate, chopped
3¹/2 cups sugar
8 eggs
1 teaspoon vanilla extract
2¹/2 cups walnuts or pecans, lightly toasted
1³/4 cups flour
¹/2 teaspoon baking powder

Chocolate Frosting
1 cup heavy cream, scalded
1 pound bittersweet chocolate, chopped
6 tablespoons butter, cut into pieces, softened

For the brownies, melt the butter and semisweet chocolate in a heatproof bowl set over a saucepan of simmering water. Beat the sugar, eggs and vanilla in a large mixing bowl. Stir in the chocolate mixture and walnuts. Mix the flour and baking powder in a small bowl. Fold into the chocolate mixture gently; do not overmix. Pour the batter into a greased 12x16-inch baking pan. Smooth the top with a spatula. Bake at 350 degrees for 30 minutes or until a wooden pick inserted in the center comes out clean. Remove to a wire rack to cool.

For the frosting, pour the hot cream over the bittersweet chocolate in a bowl. Whisk until the chocolate melts. Add the butter and whisk until the butter melts. Spread over the cooled brownies. Cut when cool.

Yield: 4 dozen brownies

Weekends
in the
Cascades

The Cascade Mountains are made up of a string of volcanoes running from Mt. Lassen in northern California to Mt. Garibaldi in British Columbia. Oregonians thrive on the spectacularly scenic recreational adventures available in the Cascades. Extensive glaciers, dense evergreen forests, and countless lakes, streams, and waterfalls are year-round destinations. Wintertime offers skiing and snowboarding at world class resorts; cross country skiing, snowshoeing, and snowmobiling in isolated backcountry wilderness; fishing in pristine mountain lakes and streams; and hunting in forests, fields, and meadows. Summertime invites canoeing, kayaking, and swimming in the lakes and streams; hiking and mountain biking on the hundreds of miles of trails; picnicking at spectacular vistas; and camping under the firs and stars.

As the sports change with the seasons, so do the menus. The cold, snowy winter's hearty stews and savory wild game dishes served with stouts, brown ales, and deep red wines are replaced with the summer's grilled meats, fish, salads, and berries served with pale ales, pinots, and chardonnays. Whether you are dining in a cozy cabin or around a campfire, the Cascades provide intimate ambience and stunning scenery for a fabulous weekend away.

Mt. Bachelor ski mountain as seen from Sunriver Resort near Bend, Oregon

photo by Bruce Berg

Weekends in the Cascades

Contents

Hungarian Mushroom Soup

6 tablespoons butter
1¹/₂ cups chopped onions
4 teaspoons Hungarian paprika
4 teaspoons dillweed
2 teaspoons salt
1 teaspoon pepper
²/₃ cup flour
1²/₃ cups milk
2²/₃ cups water
4 cups sliced mushrooms
2 tablespoons soy sauce
2 tablespoons lemon juice
¹/₂ cup sour cream
3 tablespoons chopped fresh parsley

Melt the butter in a large saucepan. Add the onions, paprika, dillweed, salt and pepper. Sauté until the onions soften. Whisk in the flour and cook for a few minutes. Whisk in the milk and water. Add the mushrooms and bring to a boil.

Reduce the heat and simmer, stirring occasionally, for 30 minutes. Remove from the heat. Stir in the soy sauce, lemon juice, sour cream and parsley. Serve immediately.

Yield: 6 servings

Wild Mushroom Soup

Mushrooms

It was a calm, sunny morning at the coast and I knew of a trail that promised good mushroom picking. I grabbed my bucket, headed up the trail, and was immediately presented with ripe salal berries and plump juicy blackberries. Further on, I found a half dozen big fat hedgehog mushrooms, a deliciously unusual discovery. When I followed a side trail through a patch of forest, I saw in front of me an amazing site: multiple beds, 15 feet by 15 feet, of perfect chanterelles. I had hit the jackpot on this short trail.

    I hiked on to a lookout with my bucket of bounty in hand, said good morning to the ocean, checked for whales through my binoculars, and seeing none, headed back to the car. For breakfast that morning, I prepared salal berry pancakes with blackberries and syrup, and a delicious cheese omelet with hedgehog and chanterelle mushrooms.

1 pound wild meadow or chanterelle mushrooms, coarsely chopped
$1/2$ cup flour
2 tablespoons butter
1 teaspoon dried minced onion
$1^1/2$ cups milk
1 cup heavy cream
Salt and pepper to taste
Finely chopped fresh parsley (optional)

Build a medium-size fire. Combine the mushrooms and flour in a sealable plastic bag. Shake to coat the mushrooms with flour. Melt the butter in a Dutch oven over medium coals. Remove the mushrooms from the flour and add to the Dutch oven. Add about 2 tablespoons of the flour and the dried onion.

Sauté the mushrooms gently until tender; do not brown. Stir the milk in gradually. Add the cream and season with salt and pepper. Stir in the parsley and serve hot.

Note: Inedible mushrooms can be deadly. If you like the idea of wild mushroom soup but are not proficient at mushroom identification, bring some large store-bought mushrooms with you.

Yield: 4 servings

Winter White Chili

16 ounces dried Great Northern beans
2 pounds boneless chicken breasts
1 tablespoon olive oil
2 onions, chopped
4 garlic cloves, minced
2 (4-ounce) cans chopped green chiles
2 teaspoons cumin
1$^1/_2$ teaspoons oregano
$^1/_4$ teaspoon ground cloves
$^1/_4$ teaspoon black or cayenne pepper
6 cups chicken stock or broth
3 cups shredded Oregon Tillamook Cheddar cheese
Salt and pepper to taste
Sour cream, salsa and chopped fresh cilantro

Place the dried beans in a large heavy saucepan. Add enough cold water to cover by 3 inches and let stand overnight; drain.

Place the chicken in a large heavy saucepan. Add enough cold water to cover and bring to a simmer. Cook for 15 minutes or until just tender. Remove the chicken and let cool. Remove and discard the skin. Cut into cubes.

Heat the olive oil in a large heavy saucepan. Add the onions and sauté for 10 minutes or until softened. Add the garlic, chiles, cumin, oregano, cloves and $^1/_4$ teaspoon pepper. Sauté for 2 minutes. Stir in the drained beans, cooked chicken and stock and bring to a boil. Reduce the heat and simmer for 2 hours or until the beans are very tender, stirring occasionally. (The chili can be prepared to this point 1 day ahead. Cover and chill. Bring to a simmer before continuing.)

Stir 1 cup of the Cheddar cheese into the soup and cook until the cheese melts. Season with salt and pepper. Ladle into bowls. Serve with the remaining cheese, sour cream, salsa and cilantro.

Note: This chili can be made in a slow cooker and allowed to simmer all day.

Yield: 8 servings

Mountain Berry French Toast

1/2 cup hazelnuts, coarsely chopped
1 (16-ounce) loaf French bread
4 eggs
1 cup heavy cream
Ground cinnamon to taste (optional)
6 cups freshly picked berries
1/3 cup water

Build a medium-size fire. Place the chopped hazelnuts in a small skillet. Toast over low coals for 10 to 12 minutes, shaking the skillet to prevent burning.

Cut the bread into ten 2-inch slices. Whisk the eggs, cream and cinnamon in a shallow bowl. Dip the bread into the egg mixture to coat completely. Cook the bread in a lightly greased skillet over medium coals for 3 minutes per side or until golden brown. Remove to a serving plate and keep warm.

Combine the berries and water in a saucepan. Cook over low coals, stirring and crushing the berries with a spoon. Cook until reduced to the consistency of a syrup. Serve over the hot French toast and sprinkle with the toasted hazelnuts.

Yield: 5 servings

Crater Lake

A full moon casts brilliant light into the crisp, clear night and cascades its beauty off layered blankets of glistening snow. Stars dance their reflection off the dark water like pirouetting fireflies in a silent and private ballet, celestial magicians transform Wizard Island's trees into majestic stalagmites reaching to the heavens.

Steam floats skyward in no particular direction from a mug of hot cocoa. Shooting stars erupt from their abodes journeying into the cosmos, as if to honor Mount Mazama's history. Simple magnificence encountered on a flawless winter evening's solitude relaxing on the rim of Crater Lake.

Simple Outdoor Omelet with Bacon

16 slices bacon
12 eggs
Chopped chives or dried parsley flakes to taste
Coarsely chopped fresh mushrooms to taste
Salt and pepper to taste
1 cup freshly grated Parmesan cheese
8 slices bread

Build a medium-size fire. Place the bacon in a large skillet. Cook over medium coals to desired doneness. Remove to paper towels to drain. Place the drained bacon on a flat pan over very low coals to keep warm. Beat the eggs in a bowl. Stir in the chives and mushrooms. Season with salt and pepper. Add about 3/4 cup of the egg mixture to the skillet and top with 1/4 cup of the Parmesan cheese. Cook over medium coals until the eggs are cooked through and the cheese begins to soften.

Fold the omelet in half and remove to a flat pan over very low coals to keep warm. Repeat with remaining eggs and cheese until all omelets have been made. Toast the bread over low coals while the omelets are cooking. Serve the omelets with the bacon and toast.

Yield: 4 servings

Breakfast Tortillas

Sausage (bulk or diced links) to taste
2 eggs per person
Shredded Cheddar cheese to taste
Small flour tortillas
Salsa to taste

Build a medium-size fire. Cook the sausage in a skillet over medium coals until cooked through. Drain the grease from the skillet. Add the eggs and cook, stirring, until scrambled and almost done. Stir in the Cheddar cheese and cook until melted. Remove and keep warm. Wrap the tortillas in foil and warm over the coals for 5 minutes. Unwrap and lay flat on a work surface. Spoon the egg mixture onto the center of the tortillas. Top with salsa. Roll up and serve.

Note: If the tortillas are hard after being warmed, wrap in a wet paper towel to soften.

Yield: Variable

Hobo Breakfast

Camping—Forest

*The early morning birdsong
and heavy scent of pine
awakened us from peaceful
slumber. We snuck out of
our tent to avoid waking the
children and started the
campfire and coffee. Shivering
in the cold, morning mountain
air but enchanted by the
majesty of the green lush forest,
we waited an eternity for the
water to boil. Then, finally,
with a hot mug of coffee cupped
in our hands, we felt our
muscles relax with warmth.*

*We relished our moment
of solitude and listened to the
crackling fire interrupt the
steady whisper of the wind in
the trees. We watched the
chipmunks and bluejays forage
for food on the soft forest floor.
When we heard the unzipping
of sleeping bags, we smiled at
each other, took another sip of
coffee, and arose from our
fireside chairs. The kids were
up, so it was time to start
breakfast.*

Seasoned salt to taste
Butter or margarine
6 eggs
1 (26-ounce) bag frozen shredded hash brown potatoes,
   thawed
1 pound cooked sausage or chopped ham
1 onion, chopped
2 cups shredded Cheddar cheese
Salt and pepper to taste

Coat the inside of a large foil cooking bag with nonstick cooking spray. Sprinkle with seasoned salt and dot with small pats of butter.

Beat the eggs in a bowl. Pour into the bag of hash browns. Add the sausage, onion and Cheddar cheese to the bag. Squeeze the bag to mix. Pour the mixture into the foil cooking bag and spread evenly in the bag. Season with salt and pepper. Dot with additional pats of butter.

Double fold the end of the bag to seal. Cook on a grill over medium coals. Turn the bag every 5 minutes and check periodically to determine when done.

Yield: 4 to 6 servings

Sirloin and Vegetable Kabobs

1 (1-inch-thick) boneless beef top sirloin steak
1 red bell pepper, cut into 1-inch pieces
1 medium yellow squash, cut into 3/4-inch slices
8 large mushrooms
1 (1-ounce) envelope ranch salad dressing mix
2 tablespoons water
1 tablespoon vegetable oil

Cut the steak into 1x1 1/4-inch cubes. Thread the steak onto four 12-inch skewers alternately with the vegetables. Mix the ranch dressing mix, water and oil in a small bowl. Brush the mixture on the kabobs. Grill over medium coals for about 10 minutes for medium-rare, turning occasionally.

Note: If using wooden skewers, soak in water for 30 minutes before using.

Yield: 4 servings

Hobo Dinner

2 pounds ground beef
2 yellow onions, chopped
3 medium potatoes, thinly sliced
4 carrots, cut into 1-inch slices
1 (10 3/4-ounce) cream of celery soup
1 (10 3/4-ounce) can cream of mushroom soup
2 tablespoons Worcestershire sauce
2 teaspoons pepper

Build a medium-size fire. Layer the ground beef, onions, potatoes and carrots in a large foil cooking bag (or 4 small foil cooking bags). Mix the cream of celery soup, cream of mushroom soup, Worcestershire sauce and pepper in a bowl. Pour over the meat and vegetables. Double fold the end of the bag to seal. Place the bag on medium coals. Cook for 45 minutes or until the ground beef is cooked through.

Note: Pouches can be prepared ahead of time and kept on ice until ready to cook.

Yield: 4 servings

Marionberry Pork Chops

Sunriver

Sunriver Resort, located east of the Cascade Mountain Range in Oregon's high desert, offers a wide variety of activities for all ages. Bike riding is among the most popular. With thirty-seven miles of trails, the excursions are almost endless: along the Deschutes River; toward the lodge, the pools, or the lush green golf courses, the beauty of this area is best enjoyed by bicycle.

A favorite ride is to the country store to select the ingredients for dinner on the deck. Back at the cabin, the outdoor ambiance is set by nature. The smell of the Ponderosa Pines mixing with smoke from the grill, the sound of the breeze rustling the trees, and the feel of the gentle swaying of the hammock all contribute to the peacefulness of this special evening.

4 center-cut pork chops
Vegetable oil
2 tablespoons butter
$1/4$ cup chopped yellow onion
$1/2$ cup sherry
$1/3$ cup marionberry purée
$1/4$ cup currant jelly
$1/4$ cup chicken stock
1 tablespoon cornstarch
$1/2$ cup marionberries

Brown the pork chops in a small amount of oil in a skillet. Reduce the heat and cook the chops until cooked through. Remove to a serving platter and keep warm. Melt the butter in a saucepan. Add the onion and sauté until softened. Add the sherry and cook until reduced by one-third.

Mix the marionberry purée, currant jelly, chicken stock and cornstarch in a small bowl. Add to the hot sherry gradually and cook, stirring constantly, until thickened. Remove from the heat and gently fold in the marionberries. Spoon over the pork chops and serve.

Note: To make marionberry purée, process fresh or frozen marionberries in a food processor or blender until puréed. Strain through a medium sieve to remove the seeds, if desired.

Yield: 4 servings

Elk Chili

2 pounds ground elk meat
$^{1}/_{2}$ cup chopped onion
3 garlic cloves, minced
2 (14$^{1}/_{2}$-ounce) cans diced tomatoes
1 (28-ounce) can pork and beans
3 tablespoons salsa
1 tablespoon brown sugar
1 tablespoon chili powder
$^{1}/_{2}$ teaspoon garlic salt
$^{1}/_{2}$ teaspoon pepper

Cook the ground elk, onion and garlic in a large saucepan over medium heat until the ground elk is cooked through; drain. Stir in the tomatoes, pork and beans, salsa, brown sugar, chili powder, garlic salt and pepper. Bring to a boil. Reduce the heat, cover and simmer for 2 hours.

Yield: 6 to 8 servings

Baked Venison

5 venison steaks
1 teaspoon meat tenderizer
1 cup Allegro Game Tame Marinade
$^{1}/_{2}$ cup bottled Italian dressing
1 teaspoon garlic salt
$^{1}/_{2}$ teaspoon lemon pepper

Arrange the steaks in a large baking dish. Sprinkle with the meat tenderizer. Pour the marinade and Italian dressing over the steaks. Marinate in the refrigerator for 3 hours. Sprinkle with garlic salt and lemon pepper. Cover the dish with foil. Bake at 325 degrees for 25 minutes.

Yield: 5 servings

Venison Jerky

2 pounds venison, cut into $1/4$-inch strips
$1/3$ cup soy sauce
$3/4$ teaspoon pepper
2 tablespoons brown sugar
$1/3$ cup Worcestershire sauce
1 tablespoon sherry or dry wine
1 teaspoon garlic powder

Arrange the venison strips in a large baking dish. Mix the soy sauce, pepper, brown sugar, Worcestershire sauce, sherry and garlic powder in a bowl. Pour over the venison. Cover and marinate in the refrigerator for at least 24 hours.

Bake at 150 degrees, or the lowest oven setting, for 4 to 7 hours or until mostly hard and dry to the touch. Remove to paper towels to drain. Pat off beads of oil with additional paper towels. Let cool to room temperature. Pack in airtight containers and store in the freezer, if possible.

Yield: $2/3$ pound

Venison Meatballs

2 pounds ground venison
5 eggs
2 tablespoons grated Parmesan cheese
2 tablespoons bread crumbs
1 teaspoon basil
2 garlic cloves, minced
1 teaspoon salt
$1/2$ teaspoon pepper
Solid vegetable shortening

Combine the venison, eggs, Parmesan cheese, bread crumbs, basil, garlic, salt and pepper in a large bowl. Mix well with hands. Dampen hands and shape the mixture into 2-inch diameter balls. Heat the shortening in a skillet until hot. Add the meatballs. Fry until browned on all sides and cooked through. Serve with gravy or ketchup, if desired.

Yield: 6 servings

Whitewater Pan-Fried Trout Supper

1/4 cup vegetable oil
1/4 cup fresh tarragon
1/4 cup fresh lemon juice
2 (2-pound) trout, cleaned, dressed
1/2 teaspoon salt
4 lemon slices
Pepper (optional)

Build a large fire. Combine the oil and tarragon in a skillet. Heat over low coals for 20 minutes or until the oil is infused with tarragon flavor. Remove the tarragon and discard. Stir in the lemon juice.

Brush the inside of each trout with some of the flavored oil. Sprinkle with some of the salt and place 2 lemon slices inside each trout. Brush the outside of each trout with the flavored oil and sprinkle with salt. Season with pepper.

Coat a grilling basket with nonstick cooking spray. Arrange the trout in the basket. Cook over hot coals, turning every 5 minutes, until the fish flakes easily.

Yield: 4 servings

Fishing

The morning mist gently bathed my face as I watched the oarsmen and guide load the gear onto the boat and put it in the McKenzie River. Soon after, I cast my first fly. The stable design of the McKenzie River boat allowed me to stand or sit while fishing. The oarsmen negotiated the whitewater skillfully. My patience was soon rewarded when I felt a tug on my line and reeled in a handsome rainbow trout.

When the boat stopped for lunch at a sandbar and the coals of the campfire burned red, my skinned trout was pan-fried. My first bite of the fresh hot trout filled my mouth with succulent flavor. Every bite thereafter tasted sensational and I knew that trout fishing in Oregon was as good as it gets.

Sautéed Chanterelles

1/4 cup olive oil
2 garlic cloves, chopped
1 1/2 pounds fresh chanterelle mushrooms, sliced
1/2 yellow onion, chopped
1 teaspoon fresh lemon juice
1/4 cup chopped fresh parsley
1 teaspoon butter
Salt and pepper to taste

Heat the olive oil in a large skillet. Add the garlic and sauté until lightly browned. Remove the garlic with a slotted spoon and set aside. Add the mushrooms and sauté for 3 minutes or until softened. Add the onion and sauté for 1 minute. Stir in the browned garlic, lemon juice, parsley and butter. Season with salt and pepper. Cook until heated through. Remove to a serving dish and serve immediately.

Yield: 6 to 8 servings

Marinated Mushrooms

1 pound fresh sliced mushrooms (such as chanterelles, king boletus or cauliflower mushrooms)
1 large sweet onion, chopped
1/2 cup olive oil
1/4 cup cider or white wine vinegar
1/2 cup honey
1/2 cup water
1/2 teaspoon salt
1/2 teaspoon oregano

Combine the mushrooms, onion, olive oil, vinegar, honey, water, salt and oregano in a saucepan. Bring to a boil. Reduce the heat and simmer gently for 10 to 15 minutes. Cover and chill. Bring to room temperature to serve.

Yield: 4 to 6 servings

Flavored Potatoes

$^1/_4$ cup olive oil

2 teaspoons lemon juice

1 teaspoon Dijon mustard

$^1/_2$ teaspoon coriander

$^1/_2$ teaspoon pepper

1 teaspoon minced onion

3 garlic cloves, minced

3 large white potatoes or 5 medium red potatoes,
   quartered, cooked

Mix the olive oil, lemon juice, mustard, coriander, pepper, onion and garlic in a bowl. Add the cooked potatoes and toss to coat. Place the potatoes in the center of a large piece of foil. Seal foil securely. Cook over medium coals until the potatoes are browned.

Note: The potato packet can be prepared ahead of time and kept on ice until ready to cook.

Yield: 4 to 6 servings

Deschutes

We secured the prime campsite with a huge grassy lawn reaching all the way to the Deschutes River bank. As the half moon rose on the crystal clear evening, we watched fish jump in the quiet purring river. The birds had quieted down, and I could no longer hear the geese or see the osprey hunting for fish. A couple of western toads hopped in around the fire.

As the sunset turned the surrounding hillside from amber to auburn, a family of deer wandered down the opposite bank looking for their evening meal. Crickets sang their evening serenade.

Potatoes and Vegetables in Foil

Melted butter
5 red potatoes, cut into bite-size pieces
1/4 cup finely chopped onion
4 large carrots
10 to 13 fresh mushrooms
4 garlic cloves, minced
2 teaspoons olive oil
Salt and pepper to taste
Butter or margarine
Oregano, basil or Tabasco sauce (optional)
Grated Parmesan cheese

Build a medium-size fire. Lay out 2 large pieces of foil to form a double layer. Brush with melted butter. Place the potatoes, onion, carrots, mushrooms and garlic on the foil. Drizzle with the olive oil. Season with salt and pepper and dot with small pats of butter. Season with oregano, basil or Tabasco sauce. Seal foil securely. Cook over medium coals for 30 minutes or until the vegetables are tender, turning a few times during cooking. Remove from the coals and open. Sprinkle with Parmesan cheese.

Yield: 6 servings

Marionberry Ice Cream

4 cups fresh or frozen marionberries
1 cup sugar
2 cups half-and-half
2 teaspoons vanilla extract

Thaw the marionberries, if frozen. Purée in a food processor or blender.

Strain through a sieve to remove the seeds. Mix the strained pulp, sugar, half-and-half and vanilla in a bowl. Cover and chill. Pour the mixture into an ice cream maker and follow the manufacturer's instructions.

Yield: 1 1/2 quarts

Berries in Citrus Yogurt Sauce

1 cup plain yogurt
1/4 cup honey
1/2 teaspoon grated lemon zest
2 teaspoons fresh lemon juice
1/2 teaspoon grated lime zest
2 teaspoons fresh lime juice
Fresh raspberries, blackberries, blueberries, strawberries
    and green grapes
Butter cookies or pieces of waffle cone

Mix the yogurt, honey, lemon zest, lemon juice, lime zest and lime juice in a small bowl. Divide the fruit between 4 goblets or parfait glasses. Spoon the sauce over the fruit and garnish with a cookie.

Note: The sauce may be prepared 1 day ahead. Cover and chill.

Yield: 4 servings

Cross-Country Skiing

We clicked into our backcountry skis and glided into the snow-laden forest. Fresh snow flocked the fir trees creating a winter wonderland. Silence hung heavy in the air, ensuring the animals a peaceful winter sleep. Except for a lone stellar bluejay that scolded us for invading his territory, we saw no animals.

A few miles later, where the forest opened onto a white glistening meadow, we stopped for lunch. The wind picked up while we ate our bagel sandwiches, so the hot mint tea we had brought along in our thermos was the perfect beverage. Rested and refueled, we raced across the meadow, out of the wind, and into the quiet sheltered forest to continue our ski through the winter paradise.

Apple Blackberry Pie

$^1/_2$ cup sugar

3 tablespoons quick-cooking tapioca

1 teaspoon grated lemon zest

$^1/_2$ teaspoon cinnamon

4 cups thinly sliced cored, peeled Granny Smith apples

3 cups blackberries

1 unbaked (9-inch) pie shell

$^1/_3$ cup marshmallow creme

2 tablespoons butter or margarine, melted

$^1/_4$ cup packed brown sugar

$^1/_2$ cup rolled oats

Mix the sugar, tapioca, lemon zest, cinnamon, apples and blackberries in a large bowl. Let stand for 15 minutes. Spoon into the pie shell. Mix the marshmallow creme, melted butter, brown sugar and rolled oats in a bowl until crumbly. Sprinkle over the fruit to within 1 inch of the edge.

Bake at 375 degrees for 60 to 70 minutes or until bubbly. Cover with foil after 45 minutes if the topping is getting too brown.

Yield: 8 servings

Rock climbers from all over the world are drawn to Smith Rock and its majestic spires and sheer walls.

Wild Blackberry Pudding Cake

1/2 cup (1 stick) butter, softened
1/2 cup sugar
1 egg
3/4 cup milk
1 cup flour
2 teaspoons baking powder
2 cups wild blackberries
3/4 cup sugar
1/2 cup cold water
Butter
Vanilla ice cream (optional)

Beat 1/2 cup butter, 1/2 cup sugar and egg in a mixing bowl until smooth. Add the milk, flour and baking powder and beat until well mixed. Spread the batter in a greased 9x9-inch baking pan.

Toss the blackberries and 3/4 cup sugar gently in a bowl. Spoon the berries evenly over the batter. Sprinkle with the cold water and dot with small pats of butter.

Bake at 450 degrees for 10 minutes. Reduce the oven temperature to 350 degrees. Bake for 30 minutes. Serve with vanilla ice cream.

Yield: 8 servings

Willamette Valley

We love to drive through the Willamette Valley farm country in late July and early August. The perfect summer sun is shining and the cool air is filled with the clean fresh scent of the harvest of the valley's mint crop. Oregon is the leading producer of mint oil in the United States, supplying almost half of the U.S. market.

Vegetarian Lifestyles

The evidence of a healthy lifestyle is visible in the face of more than one Oregonian. We enjoy hiking, biking, rollerblading, rock climbing, scuba diving, rowing, downhill and cross-country skiing, team sports, and—passionately—running. Sports enthusiasts and the slower paced alike are drawn to the vegetarian lifestyle. The natural fit is likely related to the abundance of natural food resources all over the state. One needs only to drive a short distance in any direction to find delectable, edible treasure. Oregon boasts incomparable berries, mushrooms, apples, filbert nuts, and all varieties of organic produce. Organic markets are an easy place to swap recipes and share information. Even meat lovers will find these fresh ingredients impossible to resist in the right vegetarian recipe.

Many vegetarians frequent the farmers' markets, collecting a bounty of organic fruits and vegetables. Delicious hedgehog and chanterelle mushrooms might be collected for a savory omelet. Farm-fresh squash may be used in a gratin recipe or lightly sautéed for an excellent side dish. The orchards and fruit stands are a great place to find apple cider and plump, ripe berries. Marionberries, blackberries, and salal berries all make delicious pancakes, pies, and cobblers.

Grape hyacinth wildflowers growing in a hazelnut and walnut orchard in Linn County, Oregon

photo by Steve Terrill

Vegetarian Lifestyles *Contents*

Black Bean Quesadilla

2 cups (or more) shredded Pepper Jack cheese
2 teaspoons chili powder
1 (16-ounce) can black beans, rinsed, drained
$1/3$ cup chopped green onions
$1/3$ cup chopped fresh cilantro
8 flour or corn tortillas
Salsa
Sour cream

Mix the Pepper Jack cheese, chili powder, black beans, green onions and cilantro in a bowl. Lay 1 tortilla on a work surface. Spread with $1/8$ of the cheese mixture. Top with another tortilla and spread with the cheese mixture. Continue layering to use all the tortillas and filling. Transfer to a baking sheet. Bake at 375 degrees for 10 minutes. Remove to a cutting surface. Cut into wedges and serve with salsa and sour cream.

Yield: 8 servings

Cowboy Caviar

2 tablespoons red wine vinegar
2 teaspoons hot red pepper sauce
$1^1/2$ teaspoons vegetable oil
1 garlic clove, minced
$1/8$ teaspoon ground pepper
1 avocado, peeled, pitted, cut into $1/2$-inch cubes
1 (15-ounce) can black-eyed peas, rinsed, drained
1 (11-ounce) can corn kernels
$2/3$ cup thinly sliced green onions
$2/3$ cup chopped fresh cilantro
2 to 3 Roma tomatoes, coarsely chopped
Salt to taste
Tortilla chips

Mix the vinegar, pepper sauce, oil, garlic and ground pepper in a large bowl. Add the avocado and toss gently to coat. Stir in the peas, corn, green onions, cilantro and tomatoes. Season with salt. Serve with tortilla chips. May add shredded cabbage to serve as a salad.

Yield: about 6 cups

Grilled Bread with Tomato

4 (^{1}/$_2$-inch-thick) slices hearty peasant bread
1 garlic clove, halved lengthwise
1 large ripe tomato, halved crosswise
Pinch of salt
1 tablespoon extra-virgin olive oil

Toast the bread lightly in a toaster, broiler or on an outdoor grill. Rub half the garlic clove over 2 slices of toasted bread. Then rub with half the tomato, squeezing the tomato slightly to saturate the toast with juice and pulp. Repeat with the remaining toast, garlic and tomato half. Cut each toast in half, if desired. Arrange the toasts on a serving plate. Sprinkle with salt. Drizzle with the olive oil and serve.

Yield: 4 to 8 servings

Spinach Balls

2 (10-ounce) packages frozen chopped spinach, cooked, well drained
3 cups herb-seasoned stuffing mix
1 large onion, finely chopped
6 eggs, well beaten
^{3}/$_4$ cup (1^1/$_2$ sticks) butter, melted
^{1}/$_2$ cup grated Parmesan cheese
1 tablespoon pepper
1^1/$_2$ teaspoons garlic salt
^{1}/$_2$ teaspoon thyme

Mix the spinach, stuffing, onion, eggs, melted butter, Parmesan cheese, pepper, garlic salt and thyme in a large bowl. Shape into ^{3}/$_4$-inch balls and arrange on a greased baking sheet. Bake at 325 degrees for 15 to 20 minutes.

Note: The baked spinach balls can be frozen for up to 1 month.

Yield: 24 servings

Cream of Asparagus Soup

3 pounds fresh asparagus
1/4 cup (1/2 stick) butter
1 bunch green onions, chopped
1 rib celery, finely chopped
1 quart vegetable broth
2 potatoes, peeled, cut into chunks
1/2 teaspoon lemon-herb seasoning
2 cups heavy cream
Salt and white pepper to taste

Snap off the tough lower portion of the asparagus spears and discard. Cut off the tips and set aside. Cut the remaining stalks into 1-inch pieces. Melt the butter in a large saucepan over low heat. Add the green onions and celery and sauté until the vegetables are softened. Add the broth, asparagus pieces, half the asparagus tips, potatoes and lemon-herb seasoning. Bring to a boil and skim off any foam. Reduce the heat and cover. Cook over low heat for 20 minutes or until the asparagus is tender.

Purée the soup in small batches in a food processor or blender. Strain the puréed soup into a saucepan through a sieve to remove asparagus fibers. Stir in the cream and season with salt and white pepper. Warm gently over low heat and do not let boil.

Add the reserved asparagus tips to a small saucepan of boiling salted water. Cook for 3 minutes. Plunge the asparagus tips into ice water. Drain when cool and dry with paper towels.

Ladle the soup into bowls and garnish with asparagus tips.

Yield: 6 to 8 servings

Farmer's Market

One of the favorite summer pastimes for Eugenians is visiting the farmer's market. It is so much fun to spend a morning strolling, coffee in hand, among the goods harvested from the local farms and nurseries. The senses come alive with the sights, smells, and feel of this unique mix of people and products. The brilliant hues of the just-picked flowers beckon to fill your home with color.

The pungent smell of the fresh rosemary, dill, and thyme permeate the air. The cool, smooth touch of the large juicy organic tomatoes lets your mind wander to all of the wonderful recipes waiting to be tried. The hardest part of the day will be trying to decide which items to take home and what Oregon fresh fare you will create.

Fresh Pumpkin Soup

1 large pumpkin
Vegetable oil
4 potatoes, peeled, chopped
1 garlic clove, minced
$^1/_4$ teaspoon onion powder, or a few tablespoons minced onion
Salt to taste
Vegetable or chicken broth
$^1/_4$ cup sour cream
$^1/_2$ cup (or more) milk
Pepper to taste
Chopped fresh parsley and chopped fresh thyme for garnish

Cut the top off the pumpkin. Remove the seeds and discard. Replace the top and place in a shallow baking dish. Coat the outside of the pumpkin with vegetable oil. Bake at 350 degrees for 1 hour or until softened. Remove the pumpkin to a work surface and let cool. Scoop out the cooked pumpkin, leaving enough intact to provide a sturdy bowl for the soup. Combine the pumpkin pulp, potatoes, garlic and onion powder in a saucepan. Season with salt. Add enough broth to barely cover the vegetables. Cook over medium heat for 30 minutes or until the potatoes are tender. Stir in the sour cream and milk and season with pepper. Ladle into the pumpkin shell. Garnish with chopped parsley and thyme.

Yield: 6 servings

Tortilla Soup

1 quart vegetable broth
32 ounces canned tomatoes
1 (11-ounce) can Mexicorn
1 ($8^3/_4$-ounce) can garbanzo beans
1 ($8^3/_4$-ounce) can kidney beans
1 ($8^3/_4$-ounce) can pinto beans
1 (10-ounce) can enchilada sauce
Tortilla chips
Shredded cheese

Combine the vegetable broth, tomatoes, corn, garbanzo beans, kidney beans, pinto beans and enchilada sauce in a saucepan. Bring to a boil over medium heat. Ladle into bowls and top with crushed tortilla chips and shredded cheese.

Yield: 10 servings

White Bean and Kale Soup

8 ounces dried navy beans (about 1$\frac{1}{3}$ cups)
2 tablespoons olive oil
3 ribs celery, chopped
2 carrots, peeled, sliced
1 onion, chopped
1 garlic clove, minced
6 cups canned or homemade vegetable broth
$\frac{1}{2}$ teaspoon pepper
1 bunch kale, stemmed, chopped

Place the beans in a large saucepan. Add enough water to cover the beans by 2 inches. Bring to a boil over high heat and boil for 5 minutes. Remove from the heat. Cover and let stand for 1 hour; drain.

Heat the olive oil in a large saucepan over medium-high heat. Add the celery, carrots, onion and garlic and sauté for 5 minutes. Stir in the drained beans, broth, pepper and kale. Bring to a boil over high heat. Reduce the heat and cover. Simmer for 1 hour or until the beans are tender. Remove 1 cup of beans to a bowl. Mash with a fork or potato masher. Return the mashed beans to the soup and stir to mix.

Note: You may substitute chopped fresh spinach leaves or a 10 ounce package of frozen chopped spinach in place of the kale.

Yield: 8 to 10 servings

Rainbow

I pulled my hood down further over my eyes and concentrated on the wet sidewalk as I shifted a bag of tubers and root vegetables for the evening stew from one arm to the other. Steam gently rising from the concrete in front of me told me that the sun had momentarily pushed the emptied rain clouds aside.

I looked up to the sky and saw a brilliant double rainbow majestically arching, undisturbed, from the base of the McKenzie foothills to Amazon Park. It lingered there for awhile, and not until I was home washing the stew ingredients did it melt back into the replenished rain clouds.

Blood Orange Salad

1 blood orange, peeled, cut into bite-size pieces
1 avocado, peeled, pitted, cut into $\frac{1}{2}$-inch cubes
2 green onions, finely chopped
Fresh spinach leaves, rinsed well, dried, torn
Romaine, chopped
$\frac{3}{4}$ cup olive oil
$\frac{1}{4}$ cup blood orange juice or red wine vinegar
Salt and pepper to taste

Combine the orange, avocado, green onions, spinach and romaine in a large bowl. Whisk the olive oil and blood orange juice in a small bowl. Season with salt and pepper. Add the dressing to the salad and toss gently to coat.

Yield: 4 servings

Orange, Bleu Cheese and Pecan Salad

1 bunch romaine
3 kiwifruit, peeled, sliced
1 (11-ounce) can mandarin oranges, drained
1 red onion, sliced
1/2 cup lime juice
1/4 cup olive oil
1/4 cup orange marmalade
3 tablespoons red wine vinegar
Freshly ground pepper to taste
3 ounces bleu cheese, crumbled
1/2 cup pecan halves
Croutons

Tear the romaine into bite-size pieces and place in a large bowl. Add the kiwifruit, mandarin oranges and onion. Whisk the lime juice, olive oil, marmalade and vinegar in a small bowl. Season with pepper. Toss the salad with the dressing just before serving. Top with the bleu cheese, pecans and croutons.

Yield: 8 servings

Northwest Salad

5 cups mixed salad greens
1/4 cup crumbled Gorgonzola cheese
1/4 cup sun-dried cherries
1/4 cup walnut pieces
1/4 cup grated Parmesan cheese
Bernstein's Restaurant Recipe Italian dressing

Fill a salad bowl with mixed greens. Add the Gorgonzola cheese, sun-dried cherries, walnuts, Parmesan cheese and dressing to taste. Toss lightly and top with additional Parmesan cheese.

Yield: 6 servings

Spinach Salad with Chutney Dressing

Chutney Dressing

1/4 cup wine vinegar
2 to 3 tablespoons prepared chutney
1 garlic clove, minced
2 tablespoons coarsely ground French mustard
2 teaspoons sugar
1/3 to 1/2 cup vegetable oil
Salt and pepper to taste

Salad

1 pound fresh spinach leaves, rinsed well, dried
6 mushrooms, sliced
1 cup sliced water chestnuts
6 slices bacon, cooked crisp, drained, crumbled, or an
    equivalent amount of bacon bits (optional)
3/4 cup fresh bean sprouts
1/2 cup shredded Gruyère cheese
1/4 cup thinly sliced red onion

For the dressing, combine the vinegar, chutney, garlic, mustard and
sugar in a blender or food processor container and process until smooth.
Add the oil in a fine stream, processing constantly until smooth. Add
more chutney or oil if necessary. Season with salt and pepper. Pour into
a storage container. Cover and chill. Let stand for 30 minutes at room
temperature before using.

For the salad, arrange the spinach in a salad bowl. Add the mushrooms,
water chestnuts, crumbled bacon, bean sprouts, Gruyère cheese, onion
and Chutney Dressing. Toss to coat and serve.

Note: Prepared chutney can be found in the condiment section of most
grocery stores.

Yield: 6 servings

Brewpubs

*On a cold rainy night, many
Oregonians seek refuge in the
warm ambience of a local
brewpub. The loud chatter of
patrons drowns the hiss of
falling rain. The chocolate
richness of a draught porter
warms the toes. The huge
steel or copper vats, proudly
displayed behind a glass wall,
dominate the décor.*

*Gorgeous bars reflect
Oregon's love affair with wood.
After a pint or two in the
homey brewpub, patrons are
ready to face the drizzly winter
weather again.*

Angel Hair Pasta with Roma Tomatoes and Feta

3 to 4 quarts water
Salt to taste
1 pound angel hair pasta
3 tablespoons olive oil
3 garlic cloves, minced
1 onion, chopped
2 pounds Roma tomatoes, cored, chopped
$1/2$ cup chopped fresh basil leaves
$1/4$ cup chopped fresh parsley
8 ounces feta cheese, crumbled
Salt and pepper to taste

Bring the water with salt to taste to a boil in a 6- to 8-quart saucepan. Add the pasta and cook, stirring frequently, for 3 to 5 minutes or until just tender. Drain and place in a wide, shallow serving dish.

Heat the olive oil in a 10- to 12-inch skillet over medium-high heat. Add the garlic and onion and sauté for 5 to 6 minutes or until the onion is softened. Stir in the tomatoes and cook for 2 minutes or just until warmed through. Stir in the basil and parsley and cook for 1 minute or just until the basil wilts. Pour over the pasta and add the feta cheese. Toss to mix. Season with salt and pepper. Serve hot or chilled.

Yield: 8 servings

The charming terraced patio and grassy hillside at Hinman Vineyards is a quaint setting for a family picnic.

Capellini with Fresh Tomatoes

3 large ripe tomatoes, peeled, seeded, chopped
3 garlic cloves, minced
6 oil-cured black olives, pitted, finely chopped
2 small hot chile peppers, seeded, finely chopped
1 tablespoon virgin olive oil
Juice of 1 lime
1 tablespoon chopped fresh cilantro
$1/8$ teaspoon salt
Freshly ground black pepper to taste
3 quarts water
$1^1/2$ teaspoons salt
8 ounces capellini or other thin spaghetti

Place the chopped tomatoes in a colander set over a bowl. Let drain for at least 30 minutes. Combine the drained tomatoes, garlic, black olives, chile peppers, olive oil, lime juice, cilantro and $1/8$ teaspoon salt in a large bowl. Mix well and season with pepper.

Bring the water to a boil in a large saucepan. Add the $1^1/2$ teaspoons salt and the capellini. Cook, stirring frequently, for 3 to 5 minutes or until just tender. Drain and add to the tomato mixture. Toss to mix and serve hot or chilled.

Yield: 4 servings

Flora

In April, a rainbow of tulips bloom in the Willamette Valley while irises, azaleas and rhododendrons steal the show in May. As spring turns to summer, bountiful roses bloom again and again. Then just before the vine maple sets the western slopes ablaze with fall color; dahlias are on display on the valley floor.

Shells with Roasted Vegetables

1 large red bell pepper, cored, seeded, quartered
2 medium zucchini, trimmed, halved lengthwise
1 white onion, halved
6 ribs celery, halved
8 garlic cloves
2 medium tomatoes, halved, seeded
1/4 cup olive oil
2 teaspoons Italian seasoning
2 teaspoons fennel seeds
1 cup chicken or vegetable broth
2 teaspoons Italian seasoning
1 pound pasta shells

Arrange the bell pepper, zucchini, onion, celery and garlic in a single layer in a shallow baking dish. Cover the garlic cloves with tomato halves. Drizzle the olive oil over the vegetables and sprinkle with 2 teaspoons Italian seasoning and the fennel seeds. Bake at 425 degrees for 45 to 50 minutes or until the vegetables are browned and softened. Remove the vegetables with a slotted spoon to a plate and let cool. Peel the peppers and cut the roasted vegetables into bite-sized pieces when cool.

Add the chicken broth to the baking dish. Stir and scrape the browned bits from the sides and bottom of the dish. Pour into a medium skillet and add 2 teaspoons Italian seasoning. Cook over medium heat until reduced by half.

While the liquid is reducing, add the pasta to a large pot of boiling salted water. Cook, stirring frequently, for 15 minutes or until just tender. Drain but do not rinse. Place the cooked pasta in a warmed pasta bowl and cover to keep warm.

Stir the roasted vegetables into the broth and reduce the heat. Simmer for 4 minutes or until heated through. Add to the pasta and toss to mix. Serve hot as a main course or cold as a pasta salad.

Yield: 8 servings

Red Chile and Cheese Enchiladas

1 (3-ounce) package New Mexico red chile peppers, seeded
1/4 cup vegetable oil
1 cup flour
4 to 5 cups water
1 teaspoon salt
1 teaspoon garlic powder
2 teaspoons chili powder
1 teaspoon cumin
1 teaspoon oregano
2 pounds Colby Jack or other mild cheese, shredded
1 large onion, chopped
24 corn tortillas

Place the chile peppers in a large saucepan and cover with water. Bring to a boil over medium-high heat and boil for a few minutes. Drain and place in a blender container. Blend with a small amount of water to make a paste.

Heat the oil in a large skillet. Add the flour. Cook, stirring constantly, until the flour is lightly browned. Stir in 4 or 5 cups water gradually to make a gravy consistency. Stir in the pepper paste gradually, tasting to determine the desired amount of heat. Stir in the salt, garlic powder, chili powder, cumin and oregano. Bring to a boil; remove from the heat. Spread a small amount of the red chile mixture in the bottom of each of two 9x13-inch baking dishes.

Mix the Colby Jack cheese and onion in a bowl. Heat the tortillas until softened in a skillet coated with nonstick cooking spray. Dip the tortillas in the red chile mixture and set on a work surface. Top each tortilla with a handful of the cheese mixture. Roll up the tortilla and place in a baking dish, seam side down. Sprinkle the remaining cheese mixture over the top. Bake at 350 degrees for 20 to 30 minutes or until the cheese is melted and bubbly.

Note: You may freeze the enchiladas for up to 3 weeks before baking. Let thaw before baking.

Yield: 12 servings

Lava Fields

Remarkable volcanic displays greet the traveler coming over the McKenzie Pass. Following the winding McKenzie River Valley, the highway crosses a forbidding desert of black jagged basalt. Lava fields cover an area of 85 square miles. From the Dee Wright Observatory, built atop the basaltic flood, you can enjoy a sweeping panorama of the several volcanoes involved.

Between 1964 and 1966, about a dozen NASA astronauts trained for lunar exploration on Central Oregon's volcanic landscape. Neil Armstrong, Buzz Aldrin, and others would spend the day romping around Lava Butte and the Balknap Lava Flow at McKenzie Pass in specially designed space suits.

Stuffed Pumpkin with Mushroom Gravy

1 (5-pound) pumpkin
2 cups cooked brown rice
2 cups crumbled dry corn bread
1 onion, chopped
$^1\!/_2$ cup (or more) chopped celery
2 tart apples, cored, chopped
1 cup roasted hazelnuts or cashews, coarsely chopped
Sage, thyme, marjoram and rosemary to taste
1 to 2 cups vegetable or chicken stock
2 to 4 tablespoons corn oil or melted butter
Salt and pepper to taste
Mushroom Gravy (page 137)

Cut the top off the pumpkin and set aside. Remove the seeds and stringy pulp and discard. Combine the rice, corn bread, onion, celery, apples and hazelnuts in a large bowl. Season with sage, thyme, marjoram and rosemary. Mix well with hands. Add 1 cup stock and the oil and continue mixing. Add more stock if needed to make a moist, but not wet, stuffing. Season with salt and pepper.

Pack the stuffing loosely into the pumpkin cavity. Replace the lid and bake at 325 degrees for 1$^1\!/_2$ hours or until the pumpkin flesh can be easily penetrated with a fork. Serve with Mushroom Gravy.

Note: Any excess stuffing can be baked in an oiled baking dish at 325 degrees for 1 hour.

Yield: 12 to 15 servings

Mushroom Gravy

4 ounces mushrooms, sliced
$1/4$ cup chopped onion
$1^1/2$ cups water
$1/3$ cup hazelnuts or cashews
1 tablespoon Worcestershire sauce
1 tablespoon cornstarch
1 tablespoon cold water
1 teaspoon grated fresh gingerroot

Place the mushrooms and onion in a steamer over the $1^1/2$ cups water. Steam for 5 minutes. Remove the vegetables and reserve the cooking water. Grind the hazelnuts finely in a food processor. Add $1/2$ cup of the reserved cooking water and process to mix. Remove the mixture to a small saucepan.

Stir the remaining cooking water, steamed vegetables and Worcestershire sauce into the saucepan. Bring to a simmer and cook for 3 minutes. Dissolve the cornstarch in 1 tablespoon cold water in a small cup. Add to the saucepan. Cook, stirring constantly, until the gravy thickens. Stir in the gingerroot.

Note: You may substitute $1^1/2$ cups chicken broth in place of the cooking water when making the gravy.

Yield: $1^1/2$ cups

Seasons in the Cascades

Summertime in the Cascades invites canoeing, kayaking, and swimming in the lakes and streams; hiking and mountain biking on the hundreds of miles of trails; picnicking at spectacular vistas; and camping under the firs and stars. As the sports change with the seasons, so do the menus.

The cold, snowy winter's hearty stews and savory wild game dishes served with stouts, brown ales, and deep red wine are replaced with the summer's grilled meats, fish, salads, and berries served with pale ales, pinots, and chardonnays. Whether dining in a cozy cabin or around a campfire, the Cascades provide intimate ambience and stunning scenery for a fabulous weekend away.

Summer Squash Casserole

1 pound summer squash or zucchini or a combination
$^1/4$ cup vegetable oil
$^1/2$ cup shredded Cheddar cheese
2 eggs, beaten
$^1/2$ cup finely chopped onion
$^1/2$ cup saltine or butter cracker crumbs
Celery salt, sage, salt and pepper to taste
Grated Parmesan cheese
Paprika

Trim and slice the desired squash. Steam until tender-crisp. Combine the squash, oil, Cheddar cheese, eggs, onion and cracker crumbs in a large bowl. Season with celery salt, sage, salt and pepper and mix well.

Spoon into a 9x13-inch baking dish coated with nonstick cooking spray. Sprinkle with Parmesan cheese and paprika. Bake at 350 degrees for 30 minutes.

Yield: 8 to 12 servings

Zucchini Sauté over Jasmine Rice

2 to 3 tablespoons olive oil
1 white onion, chopped
3 tablespoons chopped garlic
6 medium zucchini, trimmed, cut into $^1/2$-inch slices
4 medium tomatoes, cored, chopped
$^1/2$ cup fresh basil leaves
Salt and pepper to taste
Steamed jasmine rice

Heat the olive oil in a nonstick skillet. Add the onion and sauté over medium heat. Add the garlic when the onion is almost translucent. Sauté for 1 minute. Add the zucchini and sauté for about 2 minutes. Stir in the tomatoes and basil and season with salt and pepper. Cover and cook for 2 minutes or until the zucchini is tender-crisp. Serve over hot jasmine rice.

Yield: 8 servings

Vegetable Risotto

7 cups vegetable broth
3 tablespoons butter
1/4 cup olive oil
1 cup chopped onion
2 cups uncooked arborio rice
1 tablespoon butter
Grated Parmesan cheese to taste
Sautéed fresh vegetables such as bell peppers, garlic,
    zucchini and mushrooms

Heat the broth in a saucepan to boiling. Reduce the heat and simmer. Heat 3 tablespoons butter and the olive oil in a saucepan. Add the onion and sauté for 3 minutes. Add the rice and sauté for 2 minutes.

Stir 1 cup of hot broth into the rice mixture. Cook, stirring, until the liquid is absorbed. Add the remaining broth 1/2 cup at a time, cooking and stirring until the liquid is absorbed before adding more. Remove from the heat when all the liquid is absorbed and the rice is tender, about 15 to 20 minutes. Stir in 1 tablespoon butter and the Parmesan cheese. Remove to a serving bowl and top with the vegetables.

Note: You may add grilled shrimp or chicken for a nonvegetarian main course.

Yield: 8 servings

Cascades

When Lewis and Clark journeyed to the Pacific in 1805, they followed the Columbia River. The explorers were greatly hindered in the last stages of their trek by a series of whitewater rapids where the Columbia narrowed to run at dizzying speeds through a steep rocky gorge amid lava cliffs and roaring cataracts.

    Because the route Lewis and Clark chose was the only practical one and was consequently followed by traders and settlers, the mountains that loomed above the Columbia River rapids became known as the mountains by the cascades.

Vegetarian Calzone

Olive oil
1 green bell pepper, cut into strips
10 to 12 mushrooms, sliced
1 onion, chopped
1 (10-ounce) can refrigerated pizza dough
Cornmeal
1 (26-ounce) jar tomato and basil spaghetti sauce
6 to 8 ounces smoked mozzarella cheese, shredded, or to taste
Freshly grated Parmesan cheese

Place a pizza stone in a cold oven. Heat the oven and stone to 475 degrees.

Heat the olive oil in a skillet. Add the bell pepper, mushrooms and onion and sauté until vegetables are softened. Set aside.

Divide the pizza dough into 4 pieces. Stretch 1 piece of dough into a circle on a work surface. Transfer it to the hot pizza stone that has been sprinkled with cornmeal. Spread a few spoonfuls of spaghetti sauce on top. Top with 1/4 of the sautéed vegetables and mozzarella cheese. Sprinkle with Parmesan cheese. Drizzle with olive oil. Fold in half to make a half-moon shape. Bake at 475 degrees for 10 to 12 minutes or until golden brown. Repeat with the remaining dough, spaghetti sauce, vegetables and cheeses. Serve with warmed spaghetti sauce spooned over each calzone.

Yield: 4 calzones

How breathtakingly beautiful it is to see the panorama of the snowcapped Cascade Range, the fertile Willamette Valley and the stunning coastline from atop Mary's Peak in the coastal range.

Hazelnut Ice Cream

4 cups whole milk
1 1/4 cups sugar
1 (4-inch) piece of vanilla bean, split
1 tablespoon plus 1 1/2 teaspoons French or Italian roast
   coffee beans
5 egg yolks
2/3 cup heavy cream
2 cups hazelnuts (9 ounces)

Heat the milk, sugar, vanilla bean and coffee beans in a heavy medium saucepan. Cook, stirring constantly, for 4 to 5 minutes or until the sugar dissolves and the mixture is hot. Set aside.

Whisk the egg yolks slightly in a medium bowl. Whisk in 1 cup of the hot milk mixture, then whisk the mixture back into the saucepan. Cook over medium heat, stirring occasionally, for 8 to 10 minutes or until it reaches 175 degrees and is slightly thickened and coats the back of a spoon. Do not let the custard boil. Strain the custard through a fine sieve set over a medium bowl. Discard the vanilla bean and coffee beans. Stir in the cream and let cool to room temperature. Cover and chill completely.

Spread the hazelnuts on a baking sheet and toast at 425 degrees for about 8 minutes or until golden brown. Remove the hot nuts to a kitchen towel and rub vigorously to remove the skins. Let cool slightly. Reserve 2/3 cup of hazelnuts. Place the remaining 1 1/3 cups hazelnuts in a food processor container. Process to a paste, stopping once to scrape down the sides. Add the hazelnut paste to the chilled custard and mix well. Chop the remaining hazelnuts coarsely and fold into the mixture.

Pour the mixture into an ice cream maker and follow the manufacturer's instructions. Transfer the ice cream to a chilled container, cover tightly and freeze for up to 1 week. Let soften in the refrigerator for 30 minutes if too hard when ready to serve.

Yield: 1 1/2 quarts

Diamond Lake Innertubing

Anxious feet race, attempting to grip snow from toes enclosed in fleece-lined boots. Encumbered bodies wrapped like mummies for protection from the cold wind lumber step by step uphill. Gloved hands grip tightly to the innertube, a black rubber doughnut that propels them speeding downward. Reaching the summit, they position the projectile on the perfect pathway down the snow-covered hill. It jerks forward and suddenly scenery blurs past.

Shrieks of delight are louder than snowmobiles passing by on park trails. Gliding down, down, down, scarves flying, they reach an embankment stopping their progress. Exhilarated, they grin from ear to ear, snow-covered kids clamoring up the steep hill again for sheer sliding pleasure at Diamond Lake Resort.

Rich Gingerroot Cake

2 cups self-rising flour
1¹/₂ teaspoons grated fresh gingerroot
1 teaspoon cinnamon
¹/₂ teaspoon allspice
³/₄ cup (1¹/₂ sticks) butter, softened
¹/₂ cup packed brown sugar
1 egg
³/₄ cup molasses
³/₄ cup milk
Whipped cream or ice cream

Sift the flour with the gingerroot, cinnamon and allspice in a bowl. Beat the butter and brown sugar in a large mixing bowl until smooth. Beat in the egg and then the molasses. Beat in the dry ingredients alternately with the milk in 5 parts, beginning and ending with the dry ingredients. Pour the batter into a buttered 9-inch round, 2- to 3-inch deep cake pan. Bake at 350 degrees for 50 minutes or until a wooden pick inserted in the center comes out clean and the sides have slightly pulled away from the pan. Remove to a wire rack and let cool for 15 minutes. Serve warm with whipped cream or ice cream.

Yield: 8 servings

Filbert Clusters

2 (12-ounce) packages chocolate chips
1 (12-ounce) package butterscotch chips
1 pound roasted filberts

Place the chocolate and butterscotch chips in a microwave-safe bowl. Heat on High for 2 to 3 minutes or until melted. Stir to mix. Add the filberts and stir to coat. Drop by spoonfuls onto waxed paper and let cool.

Yield: 6 dozen clusters

Blackberry Bars

16 ounces fresh, frozen or canned blackberries
2 tablespoons plus 1$^1/_2$ teaspoons cornstarch
1 tablespoon lemon juice
1 cup all-purpose flour
1 cup whole wheat flour
2 cups quick-cooking oats
1 cup packed brown sugar
1$^1/_4$ teaspoons baking powder
$^3/_4$ teaspoon salt
$^1/_2$ teaspoon ground allspice
1 teaspoon cinnamon
1 cup (2 sticks) butter or margarine

Warm the blackberries in a medium saucepan over low heat until the juices run. (If using canned blackberries omit this step, drain the berries and reserve the juice.) Drain the juice and reserve 1 cup. Add water if necessary to make 1 cup and let cool. Combine the cooled juice, cornstarch and lemon juice in a saucepan. Cook, stirring constantly, until thickened. Stir in the blackberries gently and remove from the heat.

Mix the all-purpose flour, whole wheat flour, oats, brown sugar, baking powder, salt, allspice and cinnamon in a medium bowl. Cut in the butter until the mixture is crumbly. Spoon $^2/_3$ of this mixture into a 9x13-inch baking pan and press down.

Bake at 400 degrees for 15 minutes or until lightly browned. Let cool slightly. Spread the berry mixture over the crust. Top with the remaining flour mixture and press lightly. Bake at 400 degrees for 20 to 25 minutes or until lightly browned. Remove to a wire rack and let cool in the pan.

Yield: 8 servings

Special Occasions

Spring flowers come alive when, at winter's end, the Cascade snow melts and fills the streams and rivers. For months, Oregon showcases spectacular spring floral splendor. Picnickers flock to the lush flower gardens with their favorite outdoor foods. As summer heats up, the special occasions of bridal showers and garden weddings give way to backyard barbecues and cocktail parties.

When the kaleidoscope of colorful leaves creates a stunning canopy above, the magical season of autumn graces the Great Northwest. Families gather at orchards and pumpkin patches for fun hayrides and challenging corn mazes. Pumpkins are picked and families return home for a banquet of Grilled Gingered Pork Chops, Oven-Roasted Vegetables, and Risotto with Saffron. After the pumpkins are carved into jack-o'-lanterns, the children use the pulp for Pumpkin Chocolate Chip Cookies.

When the gray winter rains come, bountiful tables adorned with beautiful cloth, holly arrangements, fine china, and crystal welcome family and friends home for the holidays. The warm fire and savory aromas from the kitchen set the mood as the children delight in Snowflake Cookies and the adults enjoy Hot Butter Rum and Holiday Baked Brie. Laughter and good cheer last throughout the evening, the holiday season, and the New Year.

Dames rocket wildflowers on Crown Point, which overlooks the Columbia River Gorge National Scenic Area, Oregon

photo by Steve Terrill

Special Occasions Contents

Special Occasions *Menus*

Sunset Cocktail Party

Crudites platter
150   Caponata
Pita triangles
151   Gourmet Mushrooms
152   Flank Steak Pinwheels
165   Chocolate-Dipped Strawberries
White wine
Soft drinks

Backyard Barbecue

151   Fruit "Cocktail" Tidbits
158   Grilled Marinated Salmon Steak
159   Lemon and Herb Asparagus
162   Wild Rice Cakes
164   Cinnamon Ice Cream with fresh blackberries

Tailgating at the Home Game

160   Marinated Brussels Sprouts
155   Grilled Turkey Sandwiches or
Grilled kielbasa on Kaiser rolls
159   Spicy Baked Beans
166   Lemon Cake
154   Chocolate Zucchini Bread
Ice cold beer
Soft drinks

Harvest Fest

149   Beer Cheese Spread
Crackers or toast rounds
157   Grilled Gingered Pork Chops and Vegetables
160   Oven-Roasted Vegetables
161   Risotto with Saffron
170   Pumpkin Chocolate Chip Cookies

Special Occasions Menus

Spring Bridal Shower

172   Frozen Strawberry Daiquiri
153   Summer Salad
156   Crustless Quiche
     Rolls with butter
167   Old-Fashioned Cinnamon Coffee Cake
76   Fresh Fruit Tart
     Viennese coffee

Holiday Celebration

149   Holiday Baked Brie
     Relish tray
172   Cranberry Spritzer
     Roast turkey
163   Corn Bread Sausage Stuffing for Turkey
162   Fresh Cranberry Apple Relish
     Fresh steamed broccoli
     Mashed potatoes and gravy
171   Christmas Candy
169   Christmas Wreaths
170   Snowflake Cookies
173   Hot Butter Rum Mix

Beer Cheese Spread

2 cups shredded Cheddar cheese
1 cup shredded Monterey Jack cheese
2 ounces cream cheese, cut into cubes
1/4 cup freshly grated Parmesan cheese
2 garlic cloves, chopped
1/2 teaspoon dry mustard
2 drops Tabasco sauce
1 teaspoon Worcestershire sauce
1/2 cup flat beer

Combine the Cheddar cheese, Monterey Jack cheese, cream cheese, Parmesan cheese, garlic, dry mustard, Tabasco sauce, Worcestershire sauce and beer in a food processor container. Process until well mixed. Remove to a bowl or crock. Cover and chill overnight. Serve at room temperature for easy spreading.

Note: This spread can be refrigerated for up to 2 weeks.

Yield: 3 1/2 cups

Cascade Hops

In Oregon, it's not just the pure mountain water that makes for the excellent beer produced by its renowned microbrew industry. It's the hops. More than a dozen varieties grow in the Willamette Valley alone. Cascade hops, citrus-like and floral, are the signature of a craft beer from Oregon and considered the defacto standard for ales of the Pacific Northwest. Developed at Oregon State University in the mid-1950s, Cascade hops are often considered the finest in the world.

Holiday Baked Brie

1 (2-pound) wheel of Brie cheese or 4 (8-ounce) wheels of
   Brie cheese
4 (1-teaspoon) pats of butter
4 heaping tablespoons red raspberry jam
Sliced almonds (optional)

Slice the thin white rind off one of the flat sides of the Brie. Place the Brie on a baking sheet, cut side up. Bake at 400 degrees for 10 minutes or until the cheese is warm and soft. Remove to a serving plate carefully. Top with the pats of butter and let melt. Spread the jam on top and sprinkle with the almonds. Serve with warm sliced French bread.

Yield: 16 servings

Caponata

1 eggplant, unpeeled, cut into 1-inch cubes
1 tablespoon salt
2 tablespoons sugar
3 tablespoons red wine vinegar
2 tablespoons tomato paste
$^1/_4$ cup extra-virgin olive oil
$^1/_2$ large onion, coarsely chopped
1 cup diagonally sliced celery ($^1/_2$-inch slices)
$^1/_2$ green bell pepper, chopped
$^1/_2$ red bell pepper, chopped
12 pitted black olives, halved
1 cup canned crushed tomatoes in purée

Toss the eggplant and salt in a large colander. Set over a bowl and let drain for 30 to 60 minutes. Rinse the eggplant and drain well. Mix the sugar, wine vinegar and tomato paste in a small bowl. Set aside.

Heat the olive oil in a large skillet over medium heat. Add the eggplant when the oil is sizzling. Sauté the eggplant until it begins to glisten and soften. Add the onion and sauté until the eggplant is very soft. Reduce the heat and stir in the celery and bell peppers. Cover and steam for 5 to 10 minutes or until the celery and bell peppers are tender-crisp. Remove from the heat and add the tomato paste mixture, olives and tomatoes. Toss to mix.

Yield: 20 servings

Fruit "Cocktail" Tidbits

1/4 cup light rum
1/4 cup orange juice
1 teaspoon almond extract
3 to 4 cups freshly cut fruit such as melon balls, pineapple chunks,
    grapes and strawberries

Mix the rum, orange juice and almond extract in a small bowl. Place the fruit in a bowl and add the rum mixture. Toss gently to coat. Cover and chill for at least 30 minutes. Serve with toothpicks as an appetizer or in stemmed glasses as a light dessert.

Yield: 8 appetizer servings or 4 dessert servings

Gourmet Mushrooms

6 tablespoons butter
3 pounds mushrooms, trimmed
1 (12 3/4-ounce) bottle white cooking wine
2/3 cup soy sauce
Pinch of oregano
Pinch of parsley
Pinch of minced garlic
Pinch of minced onion

Melt the butter in a saucepan or slow cooker. Stir in the mushrooms, wine, soy sauce, oregano, parsley, garlic and onion. Simmer for 3 to 4 hours.

Yield: 20 servings

Flank Steak Pinwheels

8 slices peppered bacon
1 flank steak
Pepper to taste
$1/4$ cup soy sauce
$1/4$ cup Kitchen Bouquet
$1/4$ cup vegetable oil
1 tablespoon Lawry's Seasoned Salt

Cook the bacon in a skillet until cooked through but not crisp. Remove to paper towels to drain. Place the steak on a work surface and pound lightly. Season with pepper. Place the cooked bacon lengthwise on top of the steak. Roll up the steak and cut into $1^1/2$-inch slices. Secure with wooden picks.

Arrange in a single layer in a shallow dish. Mix the soy sauce, Kitchen Bouquet, oil and seasoned salt in a bowl. Pour over the steak. Cover and chill for at least 4 hours or up to 24 hours.

Remove the beef pinwheels and discard the marinade. Grill to desired doneness. Remove to a serving platter.

Yield: 12 servings

Ales

Microbreweries are part of the landscape in urban Oregon. Entrenched in the nightlife, our culture is defined by our need to create our own sustenance. It is the balance of malted grains, and the bitterness, flavor, and aroma of the hops that define a beer style. Yeast also plays an important part in the taste of some beers. Brew masters throughout the state have crafted unique, high quality brews. These masters and their crafted ales from Oregon have helped fuel the revival of the microbrew industry throughout the country.

The pinot grape is the most planted wine grape in Oregon. Chardonnay is second.

Summer Salad

Dressing
$1/2$ cup sugar
1 teaspoon salt
1 to 2 garlic cloves, minced
$1/2$ teaspoon freshly ground pepper
$1/4$ cup olive oil
$1/2$ cup red wine vinegar

Salad
1 bunch romaine
1 medium cantaloupe, peeled, seeded, cut into bite-size chunks
1 to 2 avocados, peeled, seeded, cut into bite-size chunks
$1/2$ cup chopped walnuts

For the dressing, combine the sugar, salt, garlic, pepper, olive oil and wine vinegar in a jar with a tight-fitting lid. Cover the jar and shake to mix.

For the salad, rinse the romaine and shake or spin dry. Tear into bite-size pieces and place in a large salad bowl. Add the cantaloupe, avocado and walnuts and toss gently. Add the dressing and toss to coat. Serve immediately.

Yield: 6 servings

Chocolate Zucchini Bread

Ducks Tailgating

On Saturdays during the fall, many Oregonians can be found at Autzen Stadium cheering on the Oregon Ducks football team. But it's not just the game that gets the fans to the parking lot four hours before kickoff...it's the tailgating! The parties run the gamut from beer and potato chips to fully equipped green and yellow catered affairs.

Early in the season, when the weather is still sunny and warm, hamburgers and bratwurst can be found sizzling on the open grill. As the season continues, the chill is in the air and the tailgating food of choice turns to steaming chili served with warm corn bread muffins. Whatever the weather and regardless of the score, a great time is sure to be had by all.

$1/2$ cup (1 stick) butter, softened
$1/2$ cup vegetable oil
$1^1/2$ cups sugar
2 eggs
$1/2$ cup milk
$2^1/2$ cups flour
$1/4$ cup baking cocoa
$1^1/2$ teaspoons baking powder
1 teaspoon baking soda
1 teaspoon salt
2 cups grated zucchini
1 cup chocolate chips (6 ounces)

Beat the butter, oil and sugar in a mixing bowl until light and fluffy. Beat in the eggs 1 at a time. Stir in the milk. Mix the flour, baking cocoa, baking powder, baking soda and salt in a bowl. Add the dry ingredients to the butter mixture and mix well. Stir in the zucchini.

Pour the batter into 2 greased loaf pans. Sprinkle the chocolate chips over the top of the batter in each pan. Bake at 325 degrees for 40 to 45 minutes or until a wooden pick inserted in the center comes out clean.

Yield: 2 loaves

Grilled Turkey Sandwiches

Lemon Herb Mayonnaise

$1/2$ cup mayonnaise
1 tablespoon finely chopped fresh marjoram, or
    1 teaspoon dried marjoram
$1/2$ teaspoon grated lemon zest

Turkey Sandwich

$1^{1}/4$ to $1^{1}/2$ pounds uncooked turkey breast slices
    ($1/4$-inch thick)
3 tablespoons olive oil
2 tablespoons lemon juice
6 sliced sesame hamburger buns
6 large butter lettuce leaves, washed, dried, crisped
1 large firm ripe tomato, cored, cut crosswise into 6 slices
Salt and pepper to taste

For the mayonnaise, mix the mayonnaise, marjoram and lemon zest in a small bowl. Cover and chill until ready to use.

For the sandwiches, coat the turkey slices with the olive oil and lemon juice. Place on a grill 4 to 6 inches above hot coals. Cook for 2 to 3 minutes or until white in the center and cooked through. Turn the turkey once during cooking. Place the buns, cut side down, on a cooler section of the grill. Cook until lightly toasted.

Set the toasted buns on a work surface. Place 1 lettuce leaf, 1 turkey slice and 1 tomato slice on the bottom half of each bun. Season with salt and pepper. Top with the Lemon Herb Mayonnaise and the top half of the bun.

Note: You may coat the turkey with the olive oil and lemon juice up to 4 hours ahead. Cover and chill.

Yield: 6 servings

Crustless Quiche

Lithia Park, Ashland

When most people think of Lithia Park in Ashland, they think of the water...love it or hate it. This water has a mineral-salty taste with more than twenty different kinds of minerals and acids. However, Lithia Park has much more to offer than just water.

Paths and footbridges along the lush grounds pass by mature rhododendrons, inviting shade trees, and brilliant colored flowers. Wandering along the paths beside bubbling Ashland Creek, children can be heard running and playing, others feed the ducks, and some share a family picnic. A day in Ashland's Rogue Valley wouldn't be complete without a stroll through beautiful Lithia Park.

10 eggs
$1/2$ cup flour
1 teaspoon baking powder
2 cups small curd cottage cheese
4 cups shredded Monterey Jack cheese
$1/2$ cup (1 stick) margarine, softened
1 (7-ounce) can chopped green chiles
1 pound sausage, ham or bacon, browned, drained, chopped

Beat the eggs, flour and baking powder in a large mixing bowl. Stir in the cottage cheese, Monterey Jack cheese, margarine, chiles and sausage. Pour into a buttered 9x13-inch baking dish. Bake at 350 degrees for 35 minutes or until set.

Note: This recipe may be made the night before serving. Cover and chill. The baked or unbaked quiche may also be frozen. Heat at 300 degrees until set or heated through.

Yield: 12 servings

Oregon is home to over 150 wineries each producing anywhere from a few hundred to thousands of cases of wine a year.

Grilled Gingered Pork Chops and Vegetables

Pork Chops
1/2 cup dry sherry
1/2 cup soy sauce
1/4 cup vegetable oil
2 tablespoons finely chopped fresh gingerroot
2 tablespoons maple syrup or honey
2 garlic cloves, minced
4 (1-inch thick) pork chops
1 zucchini, cut into large pieces (optional)
8 mushrooms, (optional)
15 snow peas (optional)
8 green onions, cut into large pieces (optional)

Sauce
2 teaspoons cornstarch
2 teaspoons cold water
1 cup reserved marinade

For the pork chops, whisk the sherry, soy sauce, oil, gingerroot, maple syrup and garlic gently in a bowl. Place the pork chops in a large sealable plastic bag. Add 1/2 the marinade and seal the bag. Place the zucchini, mushrooms, snow peas and green onions in a large sealable plastic bag. Add the remaining marinade and seal the bag. Chill both bags for 4 to 8 hours, turning the bags occasionally. Remove the pork chops and vegetables and reserve 1 cup of the marinade.

Thread the vegetables onto skewers if desired. Grill the pork chops and vegetables over a medium-hot fire until cooked through.

For the sauce, dissolve the cornstarch in the water in a small bowl. Pour the reserved marinade into a small saucepan. Add the dissolved cornstarch. Bring to a boil over medium heat. Cook until thick and smooth, stirring constantly. Serve with the grilled pork chops and vegetables.

Yield: 4 servings

Grilled Marinated Salmon Steak

1 (1 pound) fresh Oregon Chinook salmon steak
  (preferably line-caught)
$1/2$ cup fresh lemon juice
$1/4$ cup extra-virgin olive oil
1 tablespoon chopped fresh dill
Dash of tarragon
Dash of black pepper
Olive oil
Fresh rosemary sprigs
Fresh marjoram sprigs
Fresh sage sprigs

Place the salmon in a shallow baking dish. Mix the lemon juice, olive oil, dill, tarragon and black pepper in a bowl. Pour over the salmon and let marinate until ready to grill.

Prepare the fire and brush the grill lightly with olive oil. Sprinkle the fire lightly with the rosemary sprigs. Sprinkle the fire lightly with the marjoram and sage sprigs just before grilling.

Remove the salmon from the marinade and place on the grill. Cook for 5 to 7 minutes per side or until the fish flakes easily. Baste while grilling with the marinade. Discard any unused marinade.

Yield: 4 servings

Lemon and Herb Asparagus

1 pound fresh asparagus
2 tablespoons butter
$^1/_2$ cup water
$^1/_4$ teaspoon salt
$^1/_2$ teaspoon lemon-herb seasoning

Snap off the tough lower portion of the asparagus spears and discard. Heat the butter in a large skillet over medium-high heat. Add the asparagus quickly. Shake the skillet to roll and sear the asparagus until dark green. Add the water and sprinkle with the salt and lemon-herb seasoning. Reduce the heat to medium and cover. Cook for 4 minutes. Uncover and cook until almost all of the water has evaporated. Serve immediately.

Yield: 4 servings

Spicy Baked Beans

1 (48- to 55-ounce) can baked beans
1 cup packed brown sugar
1 cup ketchup
1 pound bacon, cooked crisp, drained, crumbled
2 tablespoons Worcestershire sauce
1 to 2 green bell peppers, chopped
1 large onion, finely chopped
$^3/_4$ cup bottled chili sauce
$^3/_4$ cup bottled mild taco sauce
1 (15- to 18-ounce) can pineapple chunks (optional)

Mix the baked beans, brown sugar, ketchup, crumbled bacon, Worcestershire sauce, bell peppers, onion, chili sauce, taco sauce and pineapple chunks in a 4-quart saucepan or baking dish.

For the saucepan, cook, uncovered, over low heat for 2 hours. Cover and cook for 1 to 2 hours.

For the baking dish, bake, uncovered, at 325 degrees for 2 hours. Cover and bake for 1 to 2 hours.

Yield: 20 servings

Marinated Brussels Sprouts

1 (10-ounce) package frozen Brussels sprouts,
   or 2 cups fresh Brussels sprouts
1/2 cup Italian salad dressing
1 garlic clove, minced
2 tablespoons finely chopped onion
1 teaspoon dried parsley flakes
1/2 teaspoon dillseeds

Cook the Brussels sprouts in a small amount of boiling salted water in a saucepan for 5 minutes. Drain and let cool. Combine the cooked Brussels sprouts, salad dressing, garlic, onion, parsley and dillseeds in a bowl. Toss to coat. Cover and chill for 12 to 24 hours, stirring occasionally.

Yield: 6 to 8 servings

Oven-Roasted Vegetables

12 medium mushrooms
6 plum tomatoes, cored, quartered, seeded
3 small onions, quartered
5 large carrots, halved
1 tablespoon plus 1 1/2 teaspoons olive oil
1 tablespoon plus 1 1/2 teaspoons balsamic vinegar
1/2 teaspoon salt

Place the mushrooms, tomatoes, onions and carrots in a 9x13-inch baking pan. Mix the olive oil, vinegar and salt in a small bowl. Drizzle over the vegetables and toss to coat. Arrange the vegetables in a single layer. Roast at 425 degrees for 20 to 25 minutes or until tender.

Yield: 6 servings

Risotto with Saffron

2 tablespoons butter
1/4 cup thinly sliced leeks or finely chopped onion
1/4 cup chopped red bell pepper
3 cups chicken broth
1 cup uncooked arborio rice
1/2 cup shredded carrot
1 teaspoon salt
1/8 teaspoon thread saffron, crushed
1/8 teaspoon freshly ground black pepper
1 medium tomato, cored, chopped
2 tablespoons finely chopped fresh parsley
Freshly grated Parmesan cheese (optional)
Fresh parsley sprigs for garnish (optional)

Melt the butter in a 3-quart saucepan. Add the leeks and bell pepper and sauté until the leeks are softened but not browned. Stir in the chicken broth, rice, carrot, salt, saffron and pepper. Bring to a rolling boil. Reduce the heat and cover. Simmer for 15 minutes.

Remove from the heat and stir in the tomato and parsley. Cover and let stand for 5 to 8 minutes or until the rice is just tender. Serve topped with Parmesan cheese and garnished with parsley sprigs.

Yield: 6 servings

Sailing at Fern Ridge Lake

On a late summer evening at Fern Ridge Lake, the wind is just right for a leisurely sail. The crisp white main sail is hoisted and after a few minutes of maneuvering, the wind catches and the boat picks up speed. Next the jib sail is hoisted along with the vibrant colors of the spinnaker, the boat begins to keel, and your heart starts to race.

After a couple of hours of racing with the wind, the sails come down and it's time to enjoy the picnic of hors d'oeuvre and chilled chardonnay with the glorious setting of the sun. With the waves softly lapping against the hull of the boat, you vow to return one more time before the season ends.

Wild Rice Cakes

3 eggs, lightly beaten
2 tablespoons Dijon mustard
1/2 cup flour
1 teaspoon salt
1/2 teaspoon white pepper
1 teaspoon ground coriander
1 cup finely chopped green onions
3 cups cooked wild rice, chilled
2 tablespoons olive oil

Whisk the eggs, mustard, flour, salt, pepper and coriander in a large bowl until smooth. Stir in the green onions and wild rice. The mixture should hold together when scooped. Add a bit of water if necessary.

Heat a large skillet over medium heat. Brush the bottom of the skillet with some of the olive oil. Add rounded spoonfuls of the rice mixture to the skillet and flatten slightly with a spatula.

Cook for 3 to 5 minutes per side or until crisp and golden brown on both sides. Remove to a platter and keep warm in a very low oven. Continue frying with the remaining rice mixture. Serve warm.

Yield: 6 servings

Fresh Cranberry Apple Relish

1 pound fresh cranberries
1 orange, unpeeled, seeded
1 apple, unpeeled, cored, seeded
3/4 cup sugar
1/2 cup chopped walnuts

Combine 1/2 the cranberries, 1/2 the unpeeled orange, 1/2 the unpeeled apple and 1/2 the sugar in a food processor container. Process for 30 to 45 seconds. Remove to a bowl. Repeat with the remaining cranberries, orange, apple and sugar. Stir in the walnuts. Cover and chill for at least 1 hour before serving.

Yield: 8 servings

Corn Bread Sausage Stuffing for Turkey

8 ounces bulk pork sausage
2 onions, chopped
2 ribs celery, chopped
$^1/_2$ teaspoon sage
$^1/_2$ teaspoon thyme, crumbled
$^1/_2$ cup chicken broth
$^1/_4$ cup ($^1/_2$ stick) butter, melted
$^1/_2$ teaspoon salt
$^1/_2$ teaspoon pepper
1 skillet cooked corn bread, made from recipe on the cornmeal box,
   omitting the sugar

Cook the sausage in a heavy skillet over low heat until well browned, crumbly and cooked through. Remove to paper towels to drain. Discard all but 1 tablespoon of the drippings from the skillet. Add the onions and celery to the drippings and sauté for 10 minutes or until the vegetables are softened. Stir in the drained sausage, sage and thyme. Cook for 1 minute. Stir in the chicken broth, butter, salt and pepper. Cook until the butter is melted.

Crumble the corn bread into a large bowl. Add the sausage mixture and toss gently to moisten all ingredients. Set aside until ready to stuff the turkey or spoon into a baking dish. Bake at 350 degrees for 30 minutes if using a baking dish. Bake uncovered if you want a crust on top. Cover if a crust is not desired.

Yield: 8 to 10 servings

Cinnamon Ice Cream

2 cups milk
1 cup heavy cream
1/4x2-inch strip of lemon zest
1/2 teaspoon cinnamon
4 egg yolks
1/2 cup sugar

Combine the milk, cream, lemon zest and cinnamon in a medium saucepan and mix well. Warm over medium heat for 5 minutes or until small bubbles appear around the edges of the pan. Set aside and let cool slightly.

Whisk the egg yolks and sugar in a large bowl. Whisk in the hot milk mixture very gradually. Return the mixture to the saucepan. Cook over medium heat, stirring constantly with a wooden spoon for 5 minutes, or until the mixture coats the back of the spoon and reaches 175 degrees.

Strain the custard through a fine sieve into a large bowl. Let cool. Cover and chill for at least 2 hours or overnight. Pour the mixture into an ice cream maker and follow the manufacturer's instructions.

Note: The custard can be chilled quickly by setting the bowl in a larger bowl of ice for 30 minutes, stirring often.

Yield: 1 quart

In September, the hazelnuts naturally fall from the trees to the groomed orchard floor.

Chocolate-Dipped Strawberries

3¹/₂ cups whole fresh strawberries (1 pint)
1¹/₂ ounces semisweet chocolate
1¹/₂ ounces milk chocolate
2 teaspoons vegetable oil

Wash the strawberries, leaving the stems attached. Pat with paper towels to dry. Combine the semisweet chocolate, milk chocolate and oil in the top of a double boiler over barely simmering water. Heat until the chocolate is just melted, stirring constantly. Remove the double boiler from the heat and leave the top of the double boiler in place over the hot water.

Hold the strawberries by the stem and dip into the melted chocolate. Cover about ²/₃ of the berry and leave the stem end exposed. Hold the coated strawberry over the chocolate for a few seconds to allow the excess to drip back into the pan.

Place the strawberries, stem end down, on waxed paper or foil. Allow to harden before removing from the waxed paper. Serve alone or arrange on top of a layer of vanilla-flavored whipped cream in a baked pie shell.

Yield: 8 servings

Beaver State

Oregon's nickname, the Beaver State, harks back to the early years of the 19th century. Fur hats were fashionable in northeastern cities at the time, and Oregon's streams housed abundant beaver habitat.

With competition fierce among the fur companies for control of the western lands, adventurous trappers called mountain men became the first white people to know the region well. Later, when the rage for beaver hats had passed and Oregon's beaver supply was all but exhausted, the mountain men showed the early pioneers a route they had picked out in their trapping years, known as the Oregon Trail.

Lemon Cake

Strawberries

Oregon's superior strawberries benefit greatly from the region's ideal soil and climate. With mild winters, the plants rejuvenate earlier and produce a greater abundance of fruit in spring and summer. The cool summer evenings and warm sunny days help produce plumper, juicier fruit with a higher natural sugar content. Although many varieties of strawberries are grown throughout the world, Oregon strawberries have a sweetness all their own.

1 package SuperMoist yellow cake mix
1 ($3^1/_4$-ounce) package lemon instant pudding mix
4 eggs
$^2/_3$ cup vegetable oil
$^3/_4$ cup water
1 cup confectioners' sugar
$1^1/_2$ tablespoons butter, melted
1 to 2 tablespoons orange juice

Stir the cake mix and pudding mix in a large bowl. Add the eggs, oil and water and beat until well mixed. Pour into a greased 9x13-inch baking pan.

Bake at 350 degrees for 40 minutes or until a wooden pick inserted in the center comes out clean. Remove to a wire rack.

Poke holes in the top of the warm cake with a fork. Mix the confectioners' sugar, melted butter and orange juice in a small bowl until smooth. Spread over the top of the warm cake. Let cool in the pan before cutting.

Yield: 12 servings

Old-Fashioned Cinnamon Coffee Cake

2$^1/_2$ cups flour
$^3/_4$ cup sugar
1 cup packed brown sugar
1 teaspoon nutmeg
$^1/_2$ teaspoon salt
$^3/_4$ cup canola oil
2 teaspoons cinnamon
1 cup minus 1 tablespoon milk
1 tablespoon lemon juice
1 egg
1 teaspoon baking soda
1 teaspoon baking powder

Mix the flour, sugar, brown sugar, nutmeg, salt and oil in a bowl until crumbly. Remove 1 cup of this mixture to a small bowl. Stir in the cinnamon and set aside.

Make sour milk by mixing the milk and lemon juice in a separate bowl. Add the sour milk, egg, baking soda and baking powder to the crumb mixture. Stir until well mixed. Spread the batter into a 9x15-inch baking pan coated with nonstick cooking spray. Sprinkle with the cinnamon crumb mixture.

Bake at 350 degrees for 30 minutes or until a wooden pick inserted in the center comes out clean. Remove to a wire rack. Cut when cool.

Yield: 12 to 15 servings

Chocolate Truffle Cake

Cake
2 egg whites
1/4 cup (1/2 stick) butter, softened
1 cup sugar
2 ounces unsweetened chocolate, melted, cooled
2 egg yolks
1/4 cup milk
1 teaspoon vanilla extract
3/4 cup self-rising flour
1 cup macadamia nuts, chopped

Truffle Mousse
1 envelope unflavored gelatin
1/3 cup water
1 1/4 cups (2 1/2 sticks) butter
1 tablespoon instant espresso coffee powder
2 cups semisweet chocolate chips
3/4 cup sugar
5 egg yolks
3 tablespoons brandy
1 (7-ounce) package Belgian-style tube cookies with chocolate
1 cup heavy cream

For the cake, preheat the oven to 350 degrees. Grease and flour a 9 1/2-inch springform pan. Beat the egg whites in a mixing bowl until soft peaks form. Cream the butter and sugar in a large mixing bowl until light and fluffy. Beat in the chocolate. Add the egg yolks 1 at a time, mixing well after each addition. Beat in the milk and vanilla. Stir in the flour. Fold in the beaten egg whites until incorporated. Fold in the nuts. Pour into the prepared pan. Bake for 35 minutes or until a wooden pick inserted in the center comes out clean. Cool on a wire rack.

For the mousse, sprinkle the gelatin over the water in a heavy 2-quart saucepan. Let stand for 2 minutes or until softened. Add the butter and espresso powder. Cook until mixture is boiling, butter melts and gelatin dissolves, stirring constantly. Chop the chocolate chips with the sugar in a food processor. Pour the boiling butter mixture into the chocolate mixture with the processor running. Process until the mixture is smooth. Add the egg yolks and brandy. Process until smooth. Return to the saucepan and cook over medium-high heat until thickened, stirring constantly. Pour into a large bowl. Place over a bowl filled with ice water. Chill until thickened, stirring frequently. Place 1/4 cup of the mousse in a pastry bag fitted with a small plain tip. Chill. Pour half of the remaining mousse over the cake.

To assemble, cut each cookie into halves crosswise. Arrange cut side down around the top edge of the mousse-topped cake. Beat the cream in a mixing bowl at high speed until stiff peaks form. Fold into the remaining chocolate mousse until incorporated. Spread over the layers. Decorate the top of the cake with the mousse in the pastry bag. Chill for 4 hours or until firm. Garnish with strawberries.

Yield: 12 servings

Springtime Strawberry Pie

1 quart strawberries
1 baked (9-inch) pie shell
1 cup sugar
2 tablespoons cornstarch
1 cup water
$1/4$ teaspoon salt
Dash of red food coloring
Whipped cream or whipped topping

Rinse the strawberries and drain on paper towels to dry. Remove the stems. Arrange the strawberries over the bottom of the pie shell.

Combine the sugar, cornstarch, water and salt in a saucepan and mix well. Cook over low heat until thickened and glossy, stirring constantly. Stir in the food coloring. Pour over the strawberries. Refrigerate, covered, until chilled. Serve with whipped cream.

Yield: 6 servings

Christmas Wreaths

$1/2$ cup (1 stick) unsalted butter
30 large marshmallows
1 teaspoon vanilla extract
$1^1/2$ teaspoons green food color
4 cups corn flakes
2 teaspoons red hot cinnamon candies

Melt the butter in a medium saucepan over medium heat. Add the marshmallows. Heat until melted, stirring constantly. Whisk in the vanilla and food color. Pour over the corn flakes in a large bowl. Stir until the corn flakes are coated.

Drop tablespoonfuls of the mixture onto waxed paper-lined baking sheets coated with nonstick cooking spray. Form into wreaths quickly using buttered fingers. Decorate the wreaths with the cinnamon candies while still warm. Let cool and store in a single layer in an airtight container.

Yield: 3 dozen wreaths

Pumpkin Chocolate Chip Cookies

1 (29-ounce) can pumpkin
3¹/₂ cups packed brown sugar
1¹/₂ cups vegetable oil
2¹/₂ teaspoons vanilla extract
5¹/₂ cups flour
1 tablespoon baking powder
1 tablespoon baking soda
1¹/₂ teaspoons salt
2 teaspoons pumpkin pie spice
1 to 2 cups mini chocolate chips

Mix the pumpkin, brown sugar, oil and vanilla in a large bowl. Mix the flour, baking powder, baking soda, salt and pumpkin pie spice in a separate bowl. Add the dry ingredients to the pumpkin mixture and stir until well combined. Stir in the chocolate chips.

Drop by tablespoonfuls 2 inches apart onto a greased cookie sheet. Bake at 350 degrees for 15 minutes. Remove the cookies to a wire rack to cool.

Yield: 4 dozen

Snowflake Cookies

¹/₂ cup (1 stick) butter, softened
1 cup crunchy peanut butter
2 cups confectioners' sugar
1 cup chopped pecans
3 cups crisp rice cereal
2 cups confectioners' sugar
¹/₂ cup (or less) milk
1 teaspoon vanilla extract
Flaked coconut

Beat the butter, peanut butter and 2 cups confectioners' sugar in a mixing bowl until well mixed. Stir in the pecans and cereal. Form into balls and arrange on a platter or baking sheet. Chill until firm.

Beat 2 cups confectioners' sugar, milk and vanilla in a bowl until smooth. Spread the coconut in a shallow bowl. Roll the chilled balls in the confectioners' sugar icing and then in the coconut.

Yield: 3 dozen

Christmas Candy

1¹/₂ cups shelled raw unsalted pistachios
1¹/₂ cups dried cranberries (6 ounces)
20 ounces white chocolate, finely chopped

Place the pistachios in a pie pan. Bake at 350 degrees for 10 minutes, stirring occasionally. Do not overcook or the pistachios will lose their bright green color. Set aside and let cool.

Place a steamer basket over ¹/₂ inch of water in a medium saucepan. Bring to a boil over medium-high heat. Add the cranberries to the basket and cover. Steam for 3 minutes or until softened and moist. Remove the berries to paper towels to drain. Blot dry and let cool.

Reduce the heat to medium-low under the saucepan to keep the water at a simmer. Place ³/₄ of the white chocolate in a heatproof bowl and set over the simmering water. Heat the chocolate for 4 minutes or until two-thirds melted, stirring occasionally. Remove the bowl and add the remaining chocolate. Whisk until all the chocolate is melted and smooth. Insert a candy thermometer in the chocolate and let cool to 82 degrees, stirring occasionally. Stir in the pistachios and cranberries.

Pour the mixture onto a large baking sheet lined with parchment paper, waxed paper or foil. Spread to a 10x14-inch rectangle about ³/₈ inch thick. Chill for 20 to 30 minutes or until hardened. Break into large pieces and store in an airtight container.

Yield: 2 pounds

Hayward Field

Hayward Field is famous among track aficionados and is home to a program rich in history and tradition. Named after the first head track coach at the University of Oregon, Hayward Field was built in 1919 as a football stadium. A six-lane cinder track was added in 1921.

Many exciting events have taken place on this world-renowned track including three Olympic trials, and National NCAA and Masters championships. Track fans have cheered on numerous talented athletes, many of them hometown favorites, including Marla Runyon, Alberto Salazar, Mary Decker Slaney, and Steve Prefontaine. In the warm, spring sunshine, the bleachers fill with fans of all ages with hopes of catching a glimpse of an up-and-coming Olympian.

Cranberry Spritzer

    1 cup cranberry juice cocktail
    1 cup ginger ale
    1 cup crushed ice

Place the cranberry juice cocktail, ginger ale and ice in a blender container. Blend on high speed for 20 seconds or until smooth.

Yield: 2 servings

Frozen Strawberry Daiquiri

    5 ounces frozen strawberries in syrup, slightly thawed
    3 ounces Rose's sweetened lime juice
    3 ounces rum
    2 ounces strawberry schnapps
    2 cups crushed ice

Place the strawberries, sweetened lime juice, rum, schnapps and crushed ice in a blender container. Blend on high speed for 30 seconds or until smooth.

Yield: 2 to 3 servings

Hot Butter Rum Mix

Mix
$^1/_2$ gallon vanilla ice cream, softened
1 pound (4 sticks) butter, softened
1 (16-ounce) package brown sugar
1 (16-ounce) package confectioners' sugar
$^1/_2$ teaspoon nutmeg
$^1/_2$ teaspoon ground cloves
$^1/_2$ teaspoon cinnamon

Hot Butter Rum
1 cup boiling water
Butter

For the mix, combine the ice cream, butter, brown sugar, confectioners' sugar, nutmeg, cloves and cinnamon in a very large bowl. Stir to mix well. Spoon into an airtight container. Cover and freeze.

For each serving, mix 2 heaping tablespoons of frozen mix with 1 cup boiling water in a mug. Top with a pat of butter and stir.

Yield: 80 servings

Microbrew Types

Oregon handcrafted microbrews, from lagers and ales to porters and stouts, have gained national acclaim. Lagers are the lightest, with smooth refreshing subtle flavors. Pale ales and amber ales are brewed with locally grown Cascade hops, and have full-bodied flavor and citrus and floral aromas. India pale Ales (IPA's) are more bitter than pale and amber ales and are often cellared in oak barrels, resulting in smooth layers of taste.

Porters have a rich, dark color and roasted flavors of mocha, chocolate, and nut. Stouts, which are thicker, blacker, and creamier than porters, have a rich, chocolate, molasses flavor with smoky overtones. Other popular beers are wheat, red, and bock. All taste delicious!

Elegant Dinners

An elegant dinner in a scenic setting or by a fire can provide an intimate backdrop for a festive gathering of friends. A beautiful table setting adds to the ambiance. Selecting the centerpiece is an excellent starting point. For outdoor elegance, foliage from the forest with an addition of grapes and lavender can make a spectacular presentation. Tying a sprig of flowers to the napkin with raffia is an inexpensive, yet elegant, touch. Candle makers all over Oregon create varieties that stand alone as art. Select candles and place amidst the centerpiece in odd numbers. Now the table is ready to be set. The sparkling crystal and shiny china will light up the table.

Guests will be delighted by the little touches such as seating cards decorated with dried leaves. Once they have settled in, it is time for the wine to be poured. A delicious Oregon wine such as a Beaux Frer merlot, or a King Estate pinot, will whet the appetite. The first course of Smoked Salmon Pâté arrives, followed by Minted Melon Salad. An Oregon sauvignon blanc complements the salad perfectly. The main course may be Rack of Lamb or Parchment-Wrapped Filbert Salmon, served with a side of Marbled Creamed Root Vegetables. The presentation may include two long chives, sliced thinly, and carefully placed in an X across the meat. A rich cabernet accompanies. Finally, the dessert, perhaps Fresh Berries with Champagne Ice, leaves the guests satiated and satisfied.

Bandon Beach on the southern Oregon coast

photo by Bruce Berg

Elegant Dinners *Contents*

Elegant Dinners *Menus*

Light Summer Dinner

182   Summer Peach Soup

Caesar salad with garlic croutons

199   Barbequed Salmon with Wine Country Butter Baste

202   Hazelnut Green Beans with Warm Gorgonzola Vinaigrette

208   Fresh Pear Sorbet

Decaffeinated coffee

Special East Indian Dinner

181   Chilled Cream of Cucumber Soup

184   Yogurt, Mint and Cucumber Salad

195   Tandoori Chicken

186   Naan

204   Spicy Lentils with Curry Sauce

205   Mint Chutney

205   Spicy Peanut Chutney

210   Almond Tart

Decaffeinated espresso

Spring Lamb Dinner

179   Creamy Salmon Spread

Crisp crackers

182   French Onion Soup

185   Fresh Orange Onion Salad

194   Rack of Lamb

205   Mint Chutney

Baby green beans

207   Hood River Valley Pear Crisp with Vanilla Cream

Mint iced tea

Caviar-Stuffed Eggs

8 eggs
$^1/_3$ cup mayonnaise
1 teaspoon vinegar
1 teaspoon prepared yellow mustard
$^1/_8$ teaspoon salt
$^1/_8$ teaspoon freshly ground pepper
2 tablespoons small capers, drained, chilled
2 tablespoons caviar, chilled

Heat the eggs in a saucepan with enough water to cover. Bring to a boil over high heat. Reduce the heat, cover and simmer for 15 to 20 minutes. Cool the eggs in cold water for a few minutes. Peel the eggs under cold running water from the tap. Halve lengthwise and remove the yolks to a food processor container. Arrange the egg white halves on a baking sheet lined with paper towels.

Process the egg yolks, mayonnaise, vinegar, mustard, salt and pepper in a food processor until smooth. Remove the mixture to a pastry bag and pipe into the egg white halves. Cover and chill. Mix the capers and caviar in a small bowl. Spoon a small amount on top of each egg half. Arrange the stuffed eggs on a serving platter and serve immediately.

Yield: 8 servings

Smoked Salmon Pâté

6 to 8 ounces smoked salmon or smoked tuna
8 ounces cream cheese, softened
Juice of $^1/_2$ (or more) lemon
2 to 3 tablespoons capers
Assorted crackers

Flake the salmon and place in a food processor container. Add the cream cheese and lemon juice. Process until almost smooth. Season with additional lemon juice, if desired and process until smooth. Remove to a bowl and stir in the capers. Serve with crackers.

Yield: 6 to 8 servings

Creamy Salmon Spread

1 (15^1/$_2$-ounce) can salmon
2 envelopes unflavored gelatin
1 teaspoon sugar
1^1/$_4$ cups mayonnaise
^{1}/$_4$ cup tomato sauce
2 tablespoons lemon juice
2 teaspoons Worcestershire sauce
^{1}/$_2$ cup finely chopped celery
2 hard-cooked eggs, chopped
2 tablespoons chopped green onions
^{1}/$_4$ teaspoon freshly ground pepper
^{1}/$_2$ cup whipping cream
Lettuce leaves
Thin cucumber slices and fresh dillweed for garnish
Assorted crackers

Drain the salmon and reserve the liquid. Flake the salmon in a bowl and set aside. Add water to the liquid to make 1 cup. Pour into a small saucepan. Sprinkle with the gelatin and sugar. Heat until the gelatin dissolves, stirring constantly. Remove from the heat and let cool.

Mix the mayonnaise, tomato sauce, lemon juice and Worcestershire sauce in a large bowl. Stir in the gelatin mixture.

Chill until partially set. Fold in the salmon, celery, chopped eggs, green onions and pepper. Beat the whipping cream in a mixing bowl until soft peaks form. Fold into the salmon mixture.

Pour into a 6-cup fish-shaped or ring mold. Cover and chill until firm. Arrange lettuce leaves on a serving plate. Unmold onto the prepared plate. Garnish with cucumber slices and fresh dillweed. Serve with crackers.

Yield: 8 to 10 servings

Oysters Rockefeller

24 fresh oysters in their shells
Rock salt
1 cup finely chopped, cooked fresh spinach leaves
1/4 cup bread crumbs
2 tablespoons finely chopped celery
2 tablespoons chopped fresh parsley
1 tablespoon chopped green onions
1/2 to 3/4 teaspoon salt
1/2 teaspoon freshly ground black pepper
1/4 teaspoon cayenne pepper
3/4 cup (1 1/2 sticks) butter, softened
1/4 cup bread crumbs
1 tablespoon butter, melted

Rinse the oysters thoroughly in cold water. Insert an oyster knife or other blunt knife between the edges of the oyster shells. Cut around the opening to pry the upper flat shell from the bottom shell. Discard the upper shells. Loosen and remove the oysters from the bottom shell with the knife. Remove and discard any bits of shell that may cling to the oyster. Rinse and dry the bottom shells. Place each oyster in a bottom shell. Arrange on a layer of rock salt in a shallow baking pan.

Combine the spinach, 1/4 cup bread crumbs, celery, parsley, green onions, salt, black pepper and cayenne pepper in a bowl. Add 3/4 cup softened butter. Beat until well mixed. Spoon about 1 tablespoon of the mixture on top of each oyster. Mix 1/4 cup bread crumbs with 1 tablespoon melted butter in a small bowl. Sprinkle some on top of each oyster. Bake at 450 degrees for 10 to 12 minutes or until the bread crumbs are golden brown and the edges of the oysters begin to curl.

Yield: 6 to 8 servings

Chilled Cream of Cucumber Soup

6 medium unpeeled cucumbers,
  cut into large chunks
2 cups plain yogurt
2 cups heavy cream
3 tablespoons fresh lemon juice
2 tablespoons finely chopped fresh dill
1 tablespoon finely chopped fresh mint
Salt and white pepper
Fresh dill or mint sprigs for garnish

Place the cucumbers, yogurt, cream, lemon juice, chopped dill and chopped mint in a food processor container. Process until the cucumbers are finely chopped. Remove to a bowl. Season with salt and white pepper.

Cover and chill for 2 to 3 hours. Ladle into chilled serving bowls and garnish with dill or mint sprigs.

Yield: 6 to 8 servings

Owens Rose Garden

A Sunday stroll through Owens Rose Garden on the south bank of the Willamette River in downtown Eugene is a favorite pastime. A plethora of brilliant color encircles the grassy lawn. Roses reach near perfection. Children chase and play hide-and-seek amongst the rose beds. Adults bend to smell the fragrant roses. Couples sit holding hands on the park benches. Picnickers dine on the lawn. The river gurgles nearby. Peace and tranquility fill the soul.

Hang gliding off Cape Lookout offers a spectacular view of the peninsula and coastline.

French Onion Soup

1 tablespoon vegetable oil
$^{1}/_{4}$ cup ($^{1}/_{2}$ stick) butter
2 to 3 pounds onions, very thinly sliced
1 garlic clove, minced
2 tablespoons flour
$^{1}/_{4}$ teaspoon nutmeg
$^{1}/_{4}$ teaspoon salt
$^{1}/_{4}$ teaspoon pepper
2 quarts water
$^{1}/_{4}$ cup beef bouillon granules
$^{1}/_{2}$ cup white wine
8 slices of toasted buttered French bread
Shredded mozzarella cheese

Heat the oil and butter in a large saucepan. Add the onions and garlic and sauté until the vegetables are softened. Mix the flour, nutmeg, salt and pepper in a small bowl. Stir into the onions. Add the water and bouillon granules and bring to a boil. Reduce the heat and simmer for 1 hour. Stir in the wine and simmer for 30 minutes.

Ladle the soup into 8 individual ovenproof bowls. Top with the slices of French bread and sprinkle with mozzarella cheese. Place under a preheated broiler for 1 minute or until the cheese is melted and bubbly.

Yield: 8 servings

Summer Peach Soup

6 cups sliced fresh or frozen peaches, thawed
$^{1}/_{4}$ cup sugar
1 cup sour cream
1 cup light cream
3 tablespoons bourbon
Fresh mint sprigs for garnish

Purée the peaches in a food processor or blender for 30 seconds. Add the sugar, sour cream, light cream and bourbon. Process until smooth. Pour into a bowl. Cover and chill for several hours or overnight. Ladle into serving bowls and garnish with mint sprigs.

Yield: 4 servings

Herbed Fresh Tomato Soup

2 tablespoons butter
2 tablespoons olive oil
2 onions, thinly sliced
6 medium very ripe tomatoes, peeled, cut into eighths
1 (6-ounce) can tomato paste
2 tablespoons chopped fresh basil leaves,
   or 2 teaspoons dried basil
4 teaspoons chopped fresh thyme,
   or 1 teaspoon dried thyme
1 tablespoon chicken bouillon granules
$^1/_2$ teaspoon sugar (optional)
$2^1/_2$ cups water
1 teaspoon salt
$^1/_4$ teaspoon pepper
Chopped celery tops for garnish

Heat the butter and olive oil in a large saucepan until the butter melts. Add the onions and sauté until softened. Stir in the tomatoes, tomato paste, basil, thyme, bouillon granules and sugar. Mash the tomatoes slightly with a spoon. Stir in the water and bring to a boil. Reduce the heat, cover and simmer for 40 minutes.

Purée the soup 2 cups at a time in a food processor or blender. Remove puréed soup to a saucepan. Stir in the salt and pepper. Heat until hot. Ladle into serving bowls and garnish with celery tops.

Yield: 8 servings

Oregon Trail

The Oregon Trail began as an unconnected series of trails used by native Americans. Fur traders expanded the route to transport pelts to trading posts. In the 1830s, missionaries followed the still faint trail along the Platte and Snake Rivers to establish church connections in the Northwest.

   Economic and political events in the 1840s converged to start a large-scale emigration west on what was then known as "The Oregon Road." Joel Walker is credited as the first settler to make the complete trip with a family, in 1840. Large-scale migration started in 1843, when a wagon train of over 800 people with 120 wagons and 5,000 cattle made the five month journey.

Yogurt, Mint and Cucumber Salad

1¹/₄ cups plain yogurt
2 teaspoons finely chopped fresh mint
1 medium cucumber, peeled, thinly sliced
¹/₂ teaspoon paprika
Salt and sugar to taste

Mix the yogurt, mint, cucumber and paprika gently in a bowl. Season with salt and sugar. Cover and chill. Serve cold as an accompaniment with Indian and Middle Eastern meals.

Yield: 2 to 4 servings

Minted Melon Salad

¹/₃ cup sugar
¹/₂ cup water
1 tablespoon plus 1¹/₂ teaspoons chopped fresh mint,
    or 2 teaspoons dried mint
2 tablespoons orange juice
1 tablespoon lemon juice
8 cups assorted melon balls or bite-size pieces of melon,
    such as watermelon, cantaloupe and honeydew
1 cup fresh blueberries (optional)

Combine the sugar and water in a small saucepan. Bring to a boil over high heat, stirring until the sugar dissolves. Boil for 5 minutes. Place the mint in a small bowl. Pour the sugar syrup over the mint. Cover and chill for 1 hour.

Pour the mint syrup through a wire mesh strainer into a small bowl and discard the mint. Stir in the orange juice and lemon juice. Cover and chill completely. Place the melon in a large bowl. Pour the mint syrup over the melon and toss to mix. Top with the blueberries.

Yield: 8 servings

Fresh Orange Onion Salad

4 oranges
1 red onion, thinly sliced
1 teaspoon fresh oregano leaves
Pinch of salt
Freshly ground pepper to taste
1/4 cup extra-virgin olive oil
Black olives for garnish

Peel the oranges and remove all the white membrane. Cut crosswise into thin slices and remove any seeds. Arrange the orange slices on a serving platter. Arrange the onion slices on top. Sprinkle with the oregano and salt. Season with pepper. Drizzle with the olive oil. Garnish with black olives. Chill until ready to serve.

Yield: 4 servings

Basic Gourmet Salad Dressing

2/3 cup Marukan seasoned gourmet rice wine vinegar
1/3 cup grapeseed oil
1 to 2 garlic cloves, minced
Juice of 1/2 lemon
Salt and pepper to taste

Combine the wine vinegar, grapeseed oil, garlic and lemon juice in a cruet. Season with salt and pepper. Shake well and pour over mixed salad greens. For variety, add a bit of crushed orange pulp and juice and some chicken broth to the dressing or add lightly crushed raspberries or blackberries and 1 tablespoon orange juice to the dressing.

Note: For best results, do not substitute for Marukan seasoned gourmet rice wine vinegar or grapeseed oil.

Yield: 1 cup

Naan

2/3 cup (110-degree) water
1 teaspoon sugar
1 teaspoon dry yeast
2 cups sifted flour
1 teaspoon salt
6 tablespoons butter, melted
Softened butter
1/4 cup milk
2 teaspoons poppy seeds

Whisk the water, sugar and yeast in a small bowl. Let stand until foamy. Combine the flour and salt in a large bowl. Make a well in the center. Pour the yeast mixture and melted butter into the well. Spread some softened butter on your palms and mix the dough with hands until smooth and soft. Turn out on a floured surface and knead for 5 minutes. Cover with a damp cloth. Let rise in a warm place for 2 hours or until doubled in bulk.

Divide the dough into 6 portions. Roll out gently on a floured surface. Brush each portion with some of the milk and sprinkle with poppy seeds. Place on a baking sheet coated with nonstick cooking spray. Bake at 450 degrees for 12 minutes. Serve warm.

Yield: 6 servings

Marionberries are actually wild blackberries indigenous to Oregon, and are named for Marion County.

Pepper-Crusted Beef

2 garlic cloves
2 tablespoons vegetable oil
2 tablespoons Worcestershire sauce
1 tablespoon (or less) salt
2 tablespoons cracked black pepper
1 tablespoon crushed red pepper
3/4 cup chopped fresh rosemary
1 (3 1/2- to 4-pound) loin, prime rib or eye-of-round
　　beef roast
Fresh rosemary sprigs for garnish (optional)

Combine the garlic, oil, Worcestershire sauce, salt, black pepper, crushed red pepper and rosemary in a food processor container. Process for 30 to 45 seconds. Set the beef roast on a rack in a roasting pan. Rub the pepper mixture over the beef. Let stand for 2 hours at room temperature or cover and chill overnight.

Roast the meat at 500 degrees for 10 minutes or until the crust begins to brown. Reduce the oven temperature to 350 degrees. Roast for 1 1/4 hours or until a meat thermometer registers 125 degrees for medium-rare.

Remove the roast to a carving board and let stand, uncovered, for 10 minutes. Carve the beef into 1/2- to 1-inch slices. Arrange on a serving platter and garnish with rosemary sprigs.

Yield: 6 to 8 servings

Beer/Food Pairing

Beer styles go with different types of food, just as with wine. Enjoy an unusual beer such as fruit wheat or kriek with an appetizer. Lighter beers and pilsners go well with more delicate foods. Maltier brews, such as an English Brown ale or Bitter go well with beef main courses. Try a dry Stout with shellfish for a truly wonderful treat.

Grilled Tip Roast

2 teaspoons grated lime zest
1/2 cup fresh lime juice
1/2 cup chopped fresh cilantro
1/4 cup tequila
7 garlic cloves, chopped
2 teaspoons oregano
1/2 cup olive oil
1/3 cup soy sauce
2 teaspoons cumin
1 teaspoon pepper
2 (2-pound) beef loin tri-tip roasts
Cherry Tomato Relish

Whisk the lime zest, lime juice, cilantro, tequila, garlic, oregano, olive oil, soy sauce, cumin and pepper in a medium bowl. Pierce the roasts all over with a small sharp knife. Place in a large sealable plastic bag. Add the marinade and seal the bag. Chill for at least 2 hours or overnight, turning the bag occasionally.

Prepare the grill at medium-high heat. Remove the beef and discard the marinade. Grill for 10 minutes per side or until a meat thermometer registers 125 degrees for medium-rare. Remove the roast to a carving board and tent with foil. Let stand for 10 minutes. Carve the beef diagonally across the grain. Serve with Cherry Tomato Relish.

Yield: 4 servings

Cherry Tomato Relish

1/4 cup balsamic vinegar
4 teaspoons chopped fresh oregano
3/4 cup olive oil
4 green onions, finely chopped
2 tablespoons drained diced green chiles
4 cups halved cherry tomatoes
Salt and pepper to taste

Whisk the vinegar and oregano in a medium bowl. Whisk in the olive oil gradually. Stir in the green onions and diced chiles. Cover and chill for up to 6 hours. Add the tomatoes and toss to coat. Season with salt and pepper.

Yield: 4 servings

Cranberry Apple Pork Tenderloin

1 (16-ounce) can jellied cranberry sauce
1/4 cup packed brown sugar
1 McIntosh or Rome apple, peeled, cored, cubed
3 to 4 tablespoons brandy
1 tablespoon Triple Sec
1/2 teaspoon cinnamon
1/2 teaspoon nutmeg
1/4 teaspoon ground cloves
1 pork tenderloin
Orange slices and fresh parsley sprigs for garnish

Combine the cranberry sauce, brown sugar, apple, brandy, Triple Sec, cinnamon, nutmeg and cloves in a saucepan. Cook over medium heat until the apple is softened, stirring occasionally.

Place the tenderloin in a shallow baking dish. Pour the cranberry mixture over the pork. Roast at 350 degrees until a meat thermometer registers 157 degrees. Remove the tenderloin to a carving board and let stand until the meat thermometer registers 160 degrees.

Pour the pan drippings into a serving bowl. Slice the pork and arrange on a serving platter. Garnish with orange slices and parsley sprigs. Serve with the reserved pan drippings.

Note: The tenderloin with sauce can be covered and chilled before roasting.

Yield: 6 servings

Hot-Air Ballooning

As the morning air begins to warm, the rainbow-colored balloon fills with hot air and inflates above the meadow. While the pilot prepares for flight, the clients sip on mimosas and enjoy a brunch of perfectly baked pastries and vine-ripened berries. Stepping into the wicker basket, a sense of wonder and anticipation permeates the mood.

With a few blasts of the burner, the basket begins to lift off the ground with an almost motionless feel. The wildflowers and wildlife are enjoyed as the balloon sails along the lower altitudes. As the balloon floats silently and effortlessly through the pale blue sky, the beauty of this scenic adventure is captured momentarily in a photograph, and becomes a favorite treasured memory.

Pork Loin with Hot Chile Pepper Glaze

$1/2$ cup hot chiles, seeded, finely chopped
3 tablespoons honey
$1/4$ cup vegetable oil
$1/2$ cup chicken broth
2 garlic cloves, minced
$1/4$ teaspoon chopped rosemary
1 (3- to 4-pound) pork loin roast

Mix the chiles, honey, oil, broth, garlic and rosemary in a bowl. Pour into a sealable plastic bag. Add the pork loin and seal. Turn the bag a few times to coat. Chill for 4 hours or overnight.

Remove the pork to a large piece of foil. Shape the foil to form walls around the pork. Pour the marinade over and seal the foil with the pork and marinade inside. Place in a shallow roasting pan.

Bake at 350 degrees for $1^1/2$ to 2 hours or until the pork is cooked through. Remove the pork to a carving board and cover with foil to keep warm.

Pour the pan juices into a saucepan. Bring to a boil and reduce the heat. Simmer for 15 to 20 minutes or until reduced to a light glaze.

Place 1 to 2 tablespoons of glaze in the center of 8 dinner plates. Carve the roast into 1-inch slices and top the glaze with a slice of pork roast. Pour the remaining glaze into a gravy boat and pass at the table.

Note: Use a variety of chiles to determine the heat of the glaze.

Yield: 8 servings

Spiced Pork Tenderloin

    1 teaspoon coarse salt
    1/2 teaspoon white pepper
    1 garlic clove, minced
    1/4 teaspoon thyme
    Pinch of ground allspice
    2 tablespoons olive oil
    1 (12-ounce) pork tenderloin
    1/2 cup whole milk
    1/4 cup brandy
    Cherry Salsa

Mix the salt, pepper, garlic, thyme and allspice in a small bowl. Rub the mixture over the tenderloin. Wrap in plastic wrap and chill for 4 hours.

Heat the olive oil in a large ovenproof skillet over medium heat. Add the tenderloin and cook for 7 minutes or until browned on all sides. Place the skillet in the oven and roast at 325 degrees for 30 minutes or until cooked through. Remove the pork to a carving board and keep warm.

Add the milk and brandy to the hot skillet. Bring to a boil over high heat. Cook, stirring frequently, for 8 minutes or until reduced to about 1/4 cup. Slice the pork and arrange on serving plates. Top with the sauce. Serve with Cherry Salsa.

Yield: 4 servings

Cherry Salsa

    1/3 cup chopped onion
    1/3 cup chopped green bell pepper
    1/3 cup chopped green chiles
    1/3 cup chopped dried cherries
    1/3 cup red cherry jam
    1 tablespoon plus 1 1/2 teaspoons vinegar
    1 tablespoon plus 1 1/2 teaspoons chopped fresh cilantro

Mix the onion, bell pepper, chiles, dried cherries, cherry jam, vinegar and cilantro in a bowl. Cover and chill for several hours.

Yield: 4 to 6 servings

Pork Rib Roast with Pear Sauce

1 (10-pound) pork loin roast, trimmed, ribs frenched
3 garlic cloves, thinly sliced
2 tablespoons fresh thyme leaves
1 tablespoon plus 1$^{1}/_{2}$ teaspoons salt
1 tablespoon pepper
2 tablespoons olive oil
2 onions, peeled, root ends left intact, cut into wedges
4 medium Bartlett pears, halved, cored, cut into wedges
6 cups pear or apple cider
4 fresh thyme sprigs
$^{1}/_{2}$ small cinnamon stick
10 black peppercorns
1 whole clove
2 tablespoons minced shallots
$^{1}/_{2}$ teaspoon fresh thyme leaves
30 tiny cherry tomatoes for garnish

Make 20 small slits over the fatty side of the pork roast. Insert a slice of garlic in each slit. Sprinkle the 2 tablespoons thyme, salt and pepper over the roast. Cover and chill overnight.

Coat the bottom of a very large roasting pan with the olive oil. Set the roast in the pan, fat side up. Arrange the onion wedges around the roast. Roast at 400 degrees for 45 minutes. Add the pear wedges and turn to coat with the drippings. Roast for 30 minutes or until a meat thermometer inserted in the thickest part registers 160 degrees. Remove the roast to a carving board and surround with the onions and pears. Cover with foil to keep warm.

Combine the pear cider, thyme sprigs, cinnamon stick, peppercorns and clove in a saucepan. Bring to a boil over high heat. Boil for 30 minutes or until reduced to 2$^{1}/_{2}$ cups. Remove from the heat.

Drain the fat from the roasting pan. Add the shallots to the roasting pan and sauté over medium heat for 3 minutes or until softened. Stir in the reduced cider. Bring to a boil while scraping up any browned bits. Pour into a small saucepan. Simmer over medium heat for 8 minutes or until reduced to 1 cup. Stir in $^{1}/_{2}$ teaspoon thyme. Season with additional salt and pepper.

Carve the pork and arrange the chops on a platter. Arrange the roasted onions and pears around the pork. Garnish with the cherry tomatoes. Serve with the pear sauce.

Note: Ask your butcher to "french" the racks for you. This entails scraping the rib bones clean of meat, fat and gristle.

Yield: 10 servings

Flaming Crown Roast of Pork with Stuffing

1 (16-rib) crown roast of pork
Salt and pepper to taste
$^1/_4$ cup ($^1/_2$ stick) butter
3 green onions, sliced
4 large fresh mushrooms, sliced
2 tart apples, peeled, chopped
3 cups herb-seasoned stuffing mix
1 cup applesauce
3 tablespoons brandy
1 (10-ounce) jar apricot preserves
$^1/_2$ cup brandy

Season the roast with salt and pepper. Place bone ends up on a rack in a shallow roasting pan. Heat the butter in a skillet until melted. Add the green onions and sauté until tender. Add the mushrooms. Cook until tender, stirring constantly. Add the apples. Cook for 1 minute, stirring constantly. Stir in the stuffing mix, applesauce and brandy. Spoon into the center of the roast. Cover the stuffing and exposed ends of ribs with foil.

Heat the preserves and $^1/_4$ cup of the brandy in a saucepan, stirring frequently. Remove $^1/_4$ cup of the preserves mixture and reserve. Bake the roast at 325 degrees for 1 hour. Continue baking for 2 additional hours or to 160 degrees on a meat thermometer, basting with some of the remaining preserves mixture every 10 minutes.

Remove from the oven and let stand for 15 minutes. Place on a serving platter. Heat the reserved preserves mixture. Remove from the heat. Pour the remaining $^1/_4$ cup brandy over the preserves mixture. Ignite at the table and pour over the roast.

Yield: 8 servings

Rack of Lamb

2 (8-boned) frenched racks of lamb
1 teaspoon finely chopped fresh thyme leaves
1 teaspoon chopped fresh rosemary or dried rosemary
Salt and pepper to taste
1 tablespoon butter

Cut each rack of lamb in half to form 4 racks of 4 chops each. Mix the thyme and rosemary in a small bowl. Season with salt and pepper. Rub the mixture over each rack. Melt the butter in an ovenproof skillet. Add the lamb racks fat side down and sear over high heat.

Cook for 2¹/₂ minutes per side or until well browned. Place the skillet in the oven and roast at 450 degrees for 20 minutes for medium-well. Remove to a platter and let stand 5 minutes before serving.

Note: Ask your butcher to "french" the racks for you. This entails scraping the rib bones clean of meat, fat and gristle.

Yield: 4 servings

Oregon's state animal is the beaver, which is also the mascot of Oregon State University.

Tandoori Chicken

2 (2^{1}/$_{2}$- to 3-pound) chickens
2 tablespoons lemon juice
1^{1}/$_{2}$ teaspoons salt
2 tablespoons boiling water
1 teaspoon thread saffron, crushed
1 cup plain yogurt
3 garlic cloves, minced
2 tablespoons finely chopped fresh gingerroot
2 teaspoons cumin
2 teaspoons coriander
1 teaspoon paprika
^{1}/$_{2}$ teaspoon cayenne pepper
2 tablespoons butter, melted

Remove the skin from the chickens. Pat dry with paper towels. Cut deep slits in the chickens with a small knife. Mix the lemon juice and salt in a small bowl. Rub over the chickens, pressing the mixture into the slits. Pour the boiling water over the saffron in a small bowl. Let stand for 10 minutes.

Mix the yogurt, garlic, gingerroot, cumin, coriander, paprika and cayenne pepper in a bowl. Place each chicken in a large sealable plastic bag. Add half the saffron water and half the marinade to each bag. Seal and chill for 24 hours.

Remove the chickens from the bags and discard the marinade. Place the chickens on a rack in a large shallow roasting pan. Brush with the melted butter. Roast at 400 degrees for 15 minutes. Reduce the oven temperature to 350 degrees. Roast for 1^{1}/$_{2}$ hours or until the chicken is very tender and cooked through.

Serve with spicy lentils, pita bread and Chilled Cream of Cucumber Soup (page 181).

Yield: 8 servings

Sautéed Chicken in Lemon Cream Sauce

6 boneless skinless chicken breasts
Salt and pepper to taste
1/4 cup (1/2 stick) butter
2 tablespoons dry vermouth
2 teaspoons grated lemon zest
2 tablespoons fresh lemon juice
3/4 cup heavy cream
1/2 cup canned low-sodium chicken broth
1/2 cup freshly grated Parmesan cheese
Chopped fresh parsley
Lemon wedges for garnish (optional)

Place the chicken breasts between pieces of plastic wrap on a work surface. Pound the chicken lightly with a mallet to 1/2-inch thickness. Season with salt and pepper. Melt the butter in a large heavy skillet over medium-high heat. Add the chicken and sauté for 3 minutes per side or until cooked through. Remove the chicken to a platter. Cover with foil and keep warm.

Drain the skillet. Add the vermouth, lemon zest and lemon juice to the hot skillet. Bring to a boil while scraping up any browned bits. Boil for 1 minute. Add the cream, chicken broth and any juices accumulated from the cooked chicken. Cook for 8 minutes or until reduced to a sauce consistency. Stir in 1/4 cup of the Parmesan cheese and season with salt and pepper. Pour the sauce over the chicken. Sprinkle with the remaining 1/4 cup Parmesan cheese and the chopped parsley. Garnish with lemon wedges.

Yield: 6 servings

Baked Chicken and Rice in Fresh Pineapple Shell

2 fresh pineapples
3 tablespoons vegetable oil
8 ounces boneless skinless chicken breasts, diced
1/4 cup fish sauce
1/4 cup sugar
2 cups coconut milk
1/4 teaspoon white pepper
1/4 cup chopped fresh cilantro leaves
1/2 cup toasted filberts
1/2 cup raisins or other dried fruit
4 cups steamed jasmine rice
1 tablespoon chopped cilantro leaves

Cut the pineapples in half lengthwise, including the leaves. Remove the fruit, leaving enough intact to provide a sturdy shell. Place 1/2 cup of the pineapple in a blender container and blend until finely chopped. Reserve remaining pineapple for another use.

Heat the oil in a large skillet. Add the chicken and sauté until cooked through. Stir in the fish sauce, sugar, coconut milk and pepper. Cook until foamy. Add the chopped pineapple, 1/4 cup cilantro, filberts, raisins and rice. Remove from the heat and stir. Spoon into the pineapple shells. Place on a baking sheet and cover the pineapple leaves with foil to prevent burning. Bake at 350 degrees for 20 minutes. Sprinkle 1 tablespoon cilantro over the top.

Yield: 4 servings

Rock Cornish Game Hens with Grapes

2 Cornish game hens
Salt and pepper to taste
3 slices bacon, cut in half
2 tablespoons butter
2 slices bread, crusts trimmed, cut into 4 triangles
$^1/_2$ cup cognac
$^1/_2$ cup heavy cream
1 tablespoon butter
2 scallions, finely chopped
12 to 20 green seedless grapes
$^1/_2$ cup port
Dash of cayenne pepper
1 teaspoon lemon juice
Fresh watercress sprigs for garnish (optional)

Season the hens with salt and pepper. Place in a well-buttered shallow roasting pan. Cover each hen with 3 half slices of bacon. Roast at 350 degrees for 50 to 60 minutes or until cooked through. Baste frequently with the pan juices during cooking. Heat 2 tablespoons butter in a skillet until hot. Add the bread and cook until golden brown on both sides. Remove to paper towels to drain. Arrange the triangles on a hot serving platter. Remove the hens from the oven and cut in half. Place half a hen on each toast triangle. Keep warm.

Place the roasting pan over medium heat. Add the cognac and cook until reduced by half. Stir in the cream and boil until reduced to a creamy consistency. Melt 1 tablespoon butter in a small saucepan. Add the scallions and sauté for 2 minutes. Add the grapes and port and ignite immediately. Stir until the flames burn out. Strain the cream gravy from the roasting pan though a wire mesh strainer into the port sauce. Season with salt. Stir in the cayenne pepper and 1 teaspoon lemon juice. Pour the sauce over the hens on the platter. Garnish with fresh watercress sprigs.

Yield: 2 servings

Barbecued Salmon with Wine Country Butter Baste

1 tablespoon butter
2 garlic cloves, minced
$^1/_2$ cup dry white wine
7 tablespoons butter
3 tablespoons chopped fresh herbs,
    such as chives, thyme, chervil, basil and parsley
2 teaspoons grated lemon zest
1 (3- to 5-pound) Chinook or king salmon,
    butterflied with skin intact

Melt 1 tablespoon butter in a small heavy saucepan over low heat. Add the garlic and cook briefly. Stir in the wine. Cook until reduced to $^1/_2$ cup. Add 7 tablespoons butter and cook until just melted. Stir in the herbs and lemon zest and set aside.

Build a fire in a charcoal grill. Lay 8 to 10 green apple or alder wood boughs with leaves on the coals when the fire is medium-hot. Place the salmon, skin side down, on a single sheet of heavy-duty foil. Brush the salmon with the butter baste. Place the fish and foil on the grill rack over the fire. Cover the grill.

Cook for 10 to 20 minutes or until a meat thermometer inserted in the thickest part registers 140 degrees. Baste once or twice during cooking with the butter baste.

Yield: 6 to 10 servings

Parchment-Wrapped Filbert Salmon

Hazelnut oil
$^1/_2$ cup finely chopped filberts or $^1/_2$ cup hazelnut flour
4 salmon steaks
2 small carrots, peeled, cut into thin strips
1 small zucchini, cut into thin strips
1 small white onion, sliced
1 red bell pepper, cut into thin strips
2 tablespoons hazelnut liqueur
2 tablespoons fresh lime juice
2 tablespoons butter, melted

Cut eight 20-inch squares of parchment paper. Cut each square into a heart shape. Lay 4 hearts on a work surface. Brush one side of each heart with hazelnut oil. Spread the chopped filberts in a shallow bowl. Dip the salmon steaks in the filberts to coat both sides. Center on the oiled parchment hearts.

Steam the carrots, zucchini, onion and bell pepper until tender-crisp. Top each salmon steak with $^1/_4$ of the steamed vegetables. Mix the hazelnut liqueur, lime juice and melted butter in a small bowl. Drizzle over the vegetables and salmon. Top each with a second parchment heart. Fold the edges to seal and place on a baking sheet.

Bake at 450 degrees for 10 minutes per inch of salmon thickness or until the parchment hearts puff. Remove to serving plates and serve immediately.

Yield: 4 servings

Steamed Asparagus

Dill Vinaigrette Dressing
1/2 cup olive oil
2 tablespoons gourmet seasoned rice wine vinegar
2 tablespoons lemon juice
2 teaspoons finely chopped fresh dill
1/2 teaspoon salt
1 small garlic clove, minced

Asparagus
3/4 to 1 pound fresh asparagus
1 1/2 teaspoons salt

For the dressing, combine the olive oil, wine vinegar, lemon juice, dill, salt and garlic in a jar with a tight-fitting lid. Cover the jar and shake to mix. Chill until serving time.

For the asparagus, snap off the tough ends of the asparagus. Tie the asparagus spears in a bundle with sturdy string. Stand upright in a deep saucepan or asparagus cooker. Fill the saucepan with water to 2 to 3 inches from the asparagus tips. Remove the bundled asparagus. Add the salt to the water and bring to a boil.

Place the asparagus upright in the boiling water. Cook, covered, for 8 minutes or until tender-crisp. Remove the asparagus to a serving dish and remove the string. Top with Dill Vinaigrette Dressing and serve.

Yield: 4 servings

Hood To Coast

The Hood to Coast Relay is the world's largest and longest relay race, covering 195 miles from Timberline Lodge on Mount Hood to Seaside on the coast. About 900 12-person teams begin the jaunt on a Friday in late August and finish the following day. The record time is just under 15 hours and 45 minutes.

Hazelnut Green Beans with Warm Gorgonzola Vinaigrette

1 pound green beans (about 5 cups)
1^1/$_2$ teaspoons olive oil
^{1}/$_4$ cup balsamic vinegar
^{1}/$_4$ cup crumbled Gorgonzola cheese
1 tablespoon packed brown sugar
1 teaspoon chopped garlic
^{3}/$_4$ teaspoon chopped shallots
^{3}/$_4$ teaspoon chopped fresh thyme, or ^{1}/$_4$ teaspoon dried thyme
^{1}/$_2$ teaspoon chopped fresh basil leaves, or ^{1}/$_4$ teaspoon dried basil
1^1/$_2$ teaspoons olive oil
Salt and pepper to taste
^{1}/$_4$ cup chopped toasted hazelnuts

Add the beans to 6 cups of boiling lightly salted water in a saucepan. Blanch for 4 minutes. Plunge the beans into ice water. Drain when cool.

Combine the 1^1/$_2$ teaspoons olive oil, vinegar, Gorgonzola cheese, brown sugar, garlic, shallots, thyme and basil in a small saucepan. Warm over medium heat for 7 minutes or until the ingredients start to combine. Heat the 1^1/$_2$ teaspoons olive oil in a large skillet. Add the green beans and toss to coat. Season lightly with salt and pepper. Sauté for 1 to 2 minutes. Add the warmed vinaigrette and toss to coat. Sprinkle with the hazelnuts and serve.

Yield: 6 servings

Spinach with Rosemary

1 pound fresh spinach leaves (about 12 cups)
2 tablespoons butter
1 green onion, chopped
1 teaspoon finely chopped fresh parsley
^{1}/$_4$ teaspoon dried rosemary, crushed

Trim the spinach and tear into bite-size pieces. Rinse well. Simmer the spinach in a small amount of water in a large saucepan for 3 minutes. Drain well. Melt the butter in a saucepan. Add the drained spinach, green onion, parsley and rosemary. Sauté for 2 minutes or until the spinach is well coated and heated through.

Yield: 4 servings

Marbled Creamed Root Vegetables

2 potatoes, peeled, cubed
1 turnip, peeled, cubed
1 large rutabaga, peeled, cubed
4 medium carrots, peeled, sliced
4 tablespoons (1/2 stick) butter
Salt and pepper to taste
1 cup milk or cream

Place the potatoes and turnip in a medium saucepan. Cover the vegetables with salted water and bring to a boil. Reduce the heat slightly and cook for 15 to 20 minutes or until tender.

Place the rutabaga in a medium saucepan. Cover with salted water and bring to a boil. Reduce the heat slightly and cook for 10 minutes. Add the carrots and cook until both vegetables are tender. Remove both saucepans from the heat and drain separately.

Place the potatoes and turnips in a mixing bowl and the carrots and rutabaga in another mixing bowl. Divide the butter between the 2 bowls. Season both mixtures with salt and pepper.

Add about 1/2 cup milk gradually to the potato and turnip bowl while beating with an electric mixer. Beat until the consistency of mashed potatoes. Add about 1/2 cup milk gradually to the carrot and rutabaga bowl while beating with an electric mixer. Beat until the consistency of mashed potatoes.

Spoon both mixtures alternately into a large serving bowl. Run a knife through the mixture to achieve a marbled effect.

Yield: 6 servings

When seas are calm, gray whales can be spotted migrating to Baja California from December to February and back again mid-March to May.

Spicy Lentils with Curry Sauce

Lentils
1 cup lentils
3 cups water
1/2 teaspoon turmeric
2 whole hot green chiles
1 teaspoon salt

Curry Sauce
1/4 cup vegetable oil
1 onion, finely sliced
2 garlic cloves, thinly sliced
1/2 teaspoon mustard
1/2 teaspoon cumin seeds
6 curry leaves
2 whole dried hot red chiles
1 teaspoon lemon juice
Fresh cilantro leaves

For the lentils, rinse and drain the lentils. Combine the lentils, water, turmeric and green chiles in a large saucepan. Bring to a boil. Reduce the heat and simmer with the pan half covered until the lentils are soft and most of the water has evaporated. Remove from the heat and add the salt. Mash the lentils slightly to thicken the consistency. Add boiling water if the mixture is too thick. Remove to an ovenproof bowl and keep warm in a low oven.

For the sauce, heat the oil in a small skillet. Add the onion and garlic and sauté until the vegetables are golden brown. Add the mustard, cumin seeds, curry leaves and red chiles. Sauté for 2 to 3 minutes. Pour the sauce over the mashed lentils. Sprinkle with the lemon juice and cilantro leaves. Serve with Indian and Middle Eastern foods along with rice.

Yield: 6 servings

Mint Chutney

1/4 cup plain yogurt
2 tablespoons chopped fresh mint
2 small hot green chiles, seeded, finely chopped
1 teaspoon sugar
Salt to taste

Combine the yogurt, mint, chiles and sugar in a food processor container. Season with salt. Process until creamy. Remove to a small bowl. Cover and chill. Serve slightly chilled with hot spicy dishes.

Yield: 6 servings

Spicy Peanut Chutney

1 cup salted peanuts
1 hot green chile, seeded, chopped,
    or 1/2 teaspoon hot chile oil
1 tablespoon coconut cream, or 1 tablespoon honey

Combine the peanuts, chile and coconut cream in a food processor container. Process until smooth. Serve with Indian and Middle Eastern foods.

Yield: 6 servings

Fresh Berries with Champagne Ice

3/4 cup sugar
3 cups water
1 1/2 cups Champagne
2 teaspoons rose water
6 cups fresh berries such as blackberries, raspberries and sliced
    strawberries

Combine the sugar with 3 cups water in a nonreactive saucepan. Cook over medium heat, stirring constantly, for 3 minutes or until the sugar dissolves. Remove from the heat and stir in the Champagne and rose water. Pour into a nonreactive 9x13-inch baking dish. Cover and freeze for at least 4 hours or until firm.

Divide the berries between 8 dessert bowls or goblets. Top each bowl of berries with about 1/2 cup of Champagne Ice scraped out with a large spoon. Serve immediately.

Note: Rose water is available at some specialty food stores and Middle Eastern markets.

Yield: 8 servings

Flamed Strawberries

2 tablespoons honey
2 tablespoons butter
1 tablespoon orange liqueur
1 teaspoon grated orange zest
1 tablespoon water
3 cups fresh strawberries, halved
1 tablespoon warmed brandy

Combine the honey, butter, orange liqueur, orange zest and water in a chafing dish or attractive skillet. Bring to a boil and stir in the strawberries. Take to the table immediately and set on a trivet. Toss the strawberries for 30 seconds. Sprinkle with the warmed brandy and ignite immediately. Baste the strawberries with the flaming sauce until the flames die out. Spoon into individual dessert dishes and serve immediately.

Yield: 8 servings

Hood River Valley Pear Crisp with Vanilla Cream

Vanilla Cream

1¹/₂ cups heavy cream
3 tablespoons sifted confectioners' sugar
2 tablespoons brandy
1 vanilla bean, or 1 tablespoon pure vanilla extract

Pear Crisp

12 pears, peeled, cored and cut into thin wedges
1 cup sugar
³/₄ cup dry red wine or apple juice
¹/₂ cup pure maple syrup
2 tablespoons fresh lemon juice
2 tablespoons cornstarch
1 cup rolled oats
1 cup packed brown sugar
¹/₄ cup flour
¹/₂ teaspoon cinnamon
¹/₂ cup (1 stick) butter, cut into pieces

For the vanilla cream, combine the cream, confectioners' sugar and brandy in a chilled deep bowl. Split the vanilla bean lengthwise and scrape the seeds into the bowl. Reserve the bean for another use. Whisk the mixture until soft peaks form. Cover and chill until serving time.

For the crisp, mix the pears, sugar, wine, maple syrup, lemon juice and cornstarch in a large bowl. Let stand for 15 minutes. Mix the oats, brown sugar, flour and cinnamon in a medium bowl. Cut the butter in with a fork until crumbly. Arrange the pears in a greased 9x13-inch baking pan. Sprinkle the oatmeal mixture on top and press gently onto the pears. Bake at 350 degrees for 35 to 40 minutes or until bubbly and golden brown. Remove to a wire rack and let cool for 30 minutes. Serve warm with Vanilla Cream.

Yield: 12 servings

Fresh Pear Sorbet

3 pounds ripe pears
1 lemon, halved
$^2/_3$ cup sugar

Peel, halve and core the pears. Rub the cut side of the pears with a lemon half to prevent browning. Cut the pears into 1-inch chunks and place in a nonreactive saucepan. Add $^3/_4$ cup water and cover the pan. Simmer for 10 to 15 minutes or until the pears are easily pierced with a knife.

Strain the pears through a coarse sieve set over a medium bowl. Add the sugar to the hot cooking liquid. Stir until the sugar dissolves and set aside.

Purée the strained pears in a food processor. Squeeze 1 tablespoon juice from the remaining lemon half and add to the puréed pears. Add the pear cooking liquid. Process until well mixed. Remove to a bowl. Cover and chill completely. Pour the mixture into an ice cream maker and follow the manufacturer's instructions.

Yield: 6 servings

Haystack Rock

Haystack Rock at Cannon Beach claims fame as the world's third largest freestanding monolith. It is stunning to see, dominating the coastline for miles. A stroll past Haystack Rock along the beach promises to entice all the senses: from the smell of the salt air to the chill of the coastal winds, to the comfort of soft massaging sand underfoot.

The tide pools near its base attract adventurers of all ages to touch the soft caress of a sea anemone. The seagulls call out from their perch atop the monolith, but the roar of the ocean drowns the sound of their cries. The sensory buffet at Haystack Rock is always invigorating and rejuvenating.

Hazelnut Torte

6 eggs, beaten
1 cup sugar
1 cup flour
$^1/_2$ cup (1 stick) butter, melted, cooled
$^1/_2$ teaspoon vanilla extract
$^1/_2$ teaspoon almond extract
1 cup whole hazelnuts, skins removed
1$^1/_3$ cups confectioners' sugar
2 tablespoons water
$^1/_2$ teaspoon almond extract
9 tablespoons berry jam
$^1/_2$ cup whipping cream
1 tablespoon confectioners' sugar
1 tablespoon light rum
Fresh berries for garnish

Combine the eggs and sugar in the top of a double boiler set over hot but not boiling water. Cook for 10 minutes or until lukewarm, stirring constantly. Pour into a large mixing bowl. Beat at high speed for 15 minutes or until light and tripled in volume. Fold in the flour gradually. Fold in the melted butter, vanilla and $^1/_2$ teaspoon almond extract. Divide the batter between two 8$^1/_2$-inch round cake pans coated with nonstick cooking spray. Bake at 350 degrees for 25 to 30 minutes or until a wooden pick inserted in the center comes out clean. Cool in the pans for 10 minutes. Remove to a wire rack to cool completely.

Arrange the hazelnuts on a baking sheet. Bake at 300 degrees for 10 minutes or until lightly toasted. Remove and let cool. Place the cooled hazelnuts in a food processor container. Process for 1 minute or until finely ground. Add 1$^1/_3$ cups confectioners' sugar, water and $^1/_2$ teaspoon almond extract. Process for 15 seconds or until the mixture forms a ball.

Slice each cooled cake layer in half horizontally. Place 1 slice on a serving plate. Spread with $^1/_3$ of the hazelnut paste and 3 tablespoons of the jam. Repeat with the next 2 slices. Top with the final slice. Beat the whipping cream, 1 tablespoon confectioners' sugar and rum in a mixing bowl until soft peaks form. Spread over the top of the cake. Garnish with fresh berries.

Yield: 8 servings

Almond Tart

14 tablespoons (1³/4 sticks) butter, softened
2 cups finely ground almonds
1 cup sugar
4 eggs
2 tablespoons flour
1 tablespoon anise liqueur
1 (2-crust) pie pastry

Beat the butter, ground almonds and sugar in a large mixing bowl until light and fluffy. Beat in the eggs 1 at a time. Stir in the flour and anise liqueur.

Fit 1 pie pastry into the bottom of an 8-inch pie plate. Pour the filling into the pastry-lined pie plate. Top with the remaining pastry. Fold the top edge under the bottom crust to seal and crimp the rim in a zigzag pattern. Cut holes in the top crust to vent.

Place in the center of a 475-degree oven. Reduce the temperature to 375 degrees immediately. Bake for 45 to 50 minutes or until puffed and lightly browned. Remove to a wire rack and let cool to room temperature. Serve plain or with whipped cream.

Yield: 8 servings

Sand Dune

An Oregon sand dune can revitalize an afternoon. It can act as a gridiron for a family football game, pretend to be a bunker for a golfer, offer a black-diamond slope for a sandboarder, and be a soft tumbling floor for a pair of future gymnasts. Every day the wind blows the slate clean for another afternoon of play.

The Cascade Mountains, individual volcanic cones that tower above the range itself, dominate the landscape for dozens of miles in every direction.

White Chocolate Tart

Creamy Nut Pastry

$1/2$ cup (1 stick) butter, softened
2 tablespoons sugar
$1/2$ teaspoon vanilla extract
$1/8$ teaspoon salt
1 cup flour
2 tablespoons finely chopped almonds

Tart

8 ounces low-fat cream cheese, softened
$1/2$ cup finely chopped white chocolate, melted
3 cups red and green seedless grapes
$1/4$ cup apricot preserves
2 teaspoons vanilla extract
White chocolate shavings or curls

For the pastry, beat the butter, sugar, vanilla and salt in a mixing bowl until light and fluffy. Add the flour and almonds and mix until the consistency of cornmeal. Pat over the bottom and up the sides of a 9-inch tart pan. Bake at 400 degrees for 10 to 15 minutes or until lightly browned.

For the tart, beat the cream cheese in a mixing bowl until light and fluffy. Add the melted white chocolate and beat until blended. Spread the cream cheese mixture in the bottom of the Creamy Nut Pastry. Arrange a circle of green grapes around the outside edge on top of the filling. Arrange a circle of red grapes inside the green grapes, then another circle of red grapes. Continue until you reach the center. Heat the preserves in a small saucepan until melted. Strain over a small bowl. Add the vanilla to the strained preserves in the bowl and stir to mix. Brush the apricot glaze over the grapes. Sprinkle with white chocolate shavings. Chill until ready to serve.

Yield: 12 servings

Contributors and Testers

The Junior League of Eugene gratefully acknowledges each of these members and friends who contributed and tested recipes for this book.

We thank you for giving your time and culinary talents in preparing this project. We sincerely hope we have not inadvertently overlooked anyone who has contributed and supported us in our endeavor.

Laurel C. Allender

Jo Archer

Gini Armstrong

Cindy Backlund

Susan Bale

Betty Sue Bischoff

Carole J. Blancher

Anne Bogart

Sheila Bong

Cathi Cornils Busse

Toni Bye

Megan Capper

Darrelyn Coats

Jan Cornelius

Sylvia Cornell

Roxanne Crabtree

Portia Daisy

LaVonne Davis

Dr. William Detlefsen

Melba Cunningham Detlefsen

DeLise Dirks

Ava D. Dunks

Geri Dunks

Carole Elmblade

Jeannine Erving

Ruth Gaughn

Joyce Gibbons

C. A. Gilbert

Liz Gilbert

Doug Gleim

Liz Gleim

Sally Green

Diane Greenwood

Tanya Gregg

Nancy Grove

Radine J. Hallam

Sue Hamly

Tasha Hankins

Karen Hauck

Linda Hendrix

Starly Hodges

Lory Jepsen

Sally Johnston

Dorothy Jones

Betty Jongeward

Tammi Kalen

Marilyn G. Kays

Kristin Kernutt

Pat C. Kessinger

Sara Bischoff Knepper

Paula Kongsore

Lisa Korth

Melanie Krebs

Marianne Lane

Kathy Lassman

George Shannon Maddox

Lisa Marcotte

Vicki Martz

Joan Melvin

Jan Miller

Melissa Miller

Saddy Miller

Susan and David Miller

Debbie Mills

Irma Mitchell

Anne G. Moffatt

Beverly L. Mohler

Dennis Mullen

Marion Mullen

Daralyn DeHaven Murdoch

Brenda Nelson

Terry Niegel

Jill King Niles

Kathy Norman

Mary Sue Oldham

Jan Petrie

Kathy Pierce

Mrs. Virginia Harper Pittman

Heidi Hedberg Pollock

Trina C. Radcliffe

Lynn Rice

Diana H. Richardson

Ian Richardson

Sharon I. Rideout

Martha Rodman

Carolyn Rubenstein

Teresa Saxman

Kirsten Schermerhorn

Janet Scott

Penny Carpenter Shephard

Shelley Singell

Jenifer Skiles

Aaron C. Smith

Jodi Arvin Smith

Abbie Swangard

Jennifer Swords

Cathy Taylor

Dr. George Teller

Ellie Teller

Liesel Thomas

Nancy B. Thompson

Samantha Thurman

Kathleen P. Turner

Stan Turner

Sarah Wall

Fran Warren

Gretchen Weza

Cheril Wheatley

Myrna K. Wheeler

Beverly Wilkison

Hollie Williams

Dora Brown Wolfe

Leanne Wong

Joy Woodard

Chardonnay

Sauvignon Blanc

Muller Thurgau

Gewürztraminer

Pinot Gris

Riesling

Pinot Noir

Late Harvest Riesling

Sparkling

Cabernet Sauvignon

Index

Index

Index

Index

Index

Cooking from the Coast to the Cascades

_____
Name

_____
Street Address

_____
City   State   Zip

_____
Telephone

To order by mail, send to:

A Taste of Oregon

Junior League of Eugene

2839 Willamette Street

Eugene, Oregon 97405

800-364-4031 (telephone)

541-345-8823 (fax)

Your Order	Qty	Total
Cooking from the Coast to the Cascades at $24.95 per book		$
Shipping and handling at $5.00 per book		$
Total		$

Method of Payment: [   ] MasterCard   [   ] VISA

[   ] Check payable to A Taste of Oregon

_____
Account Number   Expiration Date

_____
Cardholder Name

_____
Signature

Photocopies will be accepted.